Researchin
Family History

CHRIS PATON

Cuimhnich air na daoine o'n d' thàinig thu

Remember those from whence you came

THE FAMILY HISTORY PARTNERSHIP

Published by
The Family History Partnership
PO Box 502, Bury
Lancashire BL8 9EP

First published 2010

ISBN: 978 1 906280 22 2

Printed and bound by
Information Press, Southfield Road, Eynsham
Oxford OX29 4JB

Contents

Acknowledgements

I would first like to thank Terry Walsh and Bob Boyd at the Family History Partnership for suggesting that I have a bash at writing a Scottish family history guide.

I am hugely indebted to Pete Wadley at the NAS, and Audrey Wyper at the GROS for very kindly giving of their time to look over the entire text. Dee Williams kindly looked over the section on the ScotlandsPeople Centre, whilst in New Register House, Ashley Beamer and Robin Urquhart also provided assistance. Both Bruce Gorie, Secretary to the Lyon Office, and Elizabeth A. Roads, MVO, Carrick Pursuivant of Arms, looked over the chapter on heraldry and set me right on many fronts, whilst at the Church of Jesus Christ of Latter Day Saints' Glasgow centre, Alison Spring suggested some useful additions to the chapter on LDS records. Debbie Kennett and Alasdair Mac-Donald further provided many useful comments on the DNA chapter.

Finally, a big thanks to my wife Claire, who proof read the book, and to my sons Calum and Jamie, who initially provided the inspiration for my ancestral pursuits!

Pictures

I am indebted to the following institutions for permission to use images in this book:

	Page number
The ScotlandsPeople Centre	cover, 13, 53
The Scottish Association of Family History Societies	19, 36
Discover my Past Scotland / Brightsolid	19
The Registrar General for Scotland	cover, 23, 34, 49
Birthlink	29
Deceased Online	37
Origins Network **www.originsnetwork.com**	47
FreeCEN.org.uk	54
Ancestry.co.uk	58, 79
National Archives of Scotland	62
EDINA National Data Centre, University of Edinburgh	67
FamilyTreeDNA.com	91
WorldFamilies.net and Richard M. Patton	93
The Lord Lyon King of Arms	96
The Trustees of the National Library of Scotland	102
ScotFamTree	108

Cover Illustrations

Top: The Matheson Dome, reproduced courtesy of ScotlandsPeople Centre.
Bottom left: Inverary War Memorial, *centre:* Charles Paton (family photograph)
Bottom right: OPR record, reproduced courtesy of The Registrar General for Scotland.

Introduction

What drives someone to research their family history? For myself, it was simple curiosity. Growing up in Northern Ireland, my family was only one of two listed with my surname in the phone book for the whole country. Just who were the Patons, and more to the point, where were they all? I believe that to know where you are going in life you need to know where you have already been, and on this front I didn't have a clue. So one day I reached for the genealogical shovel, and I started to dig...

I began with my paternal grandparents, who had separated when my father was very young. Raised by his mother, my dad knew very little about his own father's family. There was talk that Charlie Paton had been Belgian, evacuated from the country just prior to the First World War. My Presbyterian grandmother Jean, on the other hand, residing in the County Antrim town of Carrickfergus, was clearly as Scottish as haggis. She had an 'Amazing Grace' kitchen towel depicting a kilted piper hanging by the cooker and enough hairy Highlander dolls in her living room to prove the point.

Of course, no sooner had I decided to peel away the layers of our past than a different story began to emerge. Jean, more Scottish than Quaker's Oats, turned out to be the daughter of Ulster born migrants to Glasgow; Charlie was indeed born in Brussels, but to parents from Perthshire and Inverness. Far from being evacuated prior to the war, he had been trapped there throughout with his mother and sister, whilst his father, a shopkeeper working for a Glaswegian firm, had been forced into hiding from the Germans, eventually dying from the stress of it all in 1916. My grandfather's brother John had been subsequently interned as a civilian POW in a German internment camp, whilst his eldest brother William risked life and limb in Gallipoli with the Royal Army Medical Corps. I had never found a tale so dramatic or fascinating.

The discovery of a Scottish connection can come with many traps for the unwary. If you believed the tourist hype, we would all be connected to a clan somewhere and have a family coat of arms. It's a compelling image, but the truth doesn't always match the romantic dream. Every family history is different, and the research paths that we need to take will vary enormously. Many sources will be common to all of us, whilst others will be specific to our own individual stories. This book will outline the basic sources needed for tracing your Scottish ancestors, and suggest many ways back that you may not have yet discovered. It will point out the various resources currently available both online and in archives across the country; and along the way it will offer some useful tips, as well as debunk many myths.

Above all else, it is a beginner's guide, which I hope may help you to find the greatest story that you will ever discover – your very own.

1. *Working from the known to the unknown*

Getting started

If the golden rule in genealogy is to work from the known back to the unknown, then you first need to establish what you already know. On a piece of paper, or in a notebook, jot down the names of all of those relatives that you can think of within your immediate family, along with their spouses or partners. If you have their dates of birth or have a rough idea on how old they are, put that down also, and note where they live, what you think they might do or have once done for a living, and where they may have married or even died. At this stage it does not matter if you only know that the husband of your widowed Aunt Aggie might have been called Bill.

Once you have recorded as much as you can think of, have a go at scribbling out a basic family tree diagram with the information you now have. There are two very simple ways to try and do this. The first is to start with your earliest known ancestor at the top of the page, and to then list all of his or her descendants beneath, with a new line for each generation. Don't worry at this stage about listing the births of children in the right order, or about running out of room with lines crossing each other all over the shop. The second is to start with yourself at the bottom, and to then list on the line above who your two parents are, followed by your four grandparents on the line above that, etc.

When finished, you will now have a starting point for your research. It may be wrong on a few fronts, and it may look like something that the cat dragged in, but the very act of consigning what you already know to a page will allow you to appreciate the task that you are letting yourself in for. It will identify the limits of your family knowledge, and provide the first *aide-memoire* to get you going.

Ask the Family

Now it is time to get the family involved if you can – but a word of caution. You may well be brimming with enthusiasm about researching your family, but some of your relatives may not be. They may have stories that they don't want to share, and there could well be skeletons lurking in the closet. They may also be just completely uninterested.

If your relatives are happy to help, encourage them to dig out any old photos, certificates or other documents that might assist when you meet up. It is worth bringing a small digital camera with you to your meeting, so that you can take copies if allowed. You might also wish to bring a video camera or tape recorder along to record your chat, but my advice would be not to do so during a first visit. The act of being recorded may make your relatives feel uncomfortable, and may actually put them on the defensive.

Choose a familiar and comfortable environment, around the kitchen table or on the living room sofa, and get the kettle on. Using your tree drawing and notes, discuss your individual family members and try to gain clues as to where they may have been born or married, where they lived or what their occupations might have been. Discuss photos or documents that your relative may have that can help tell the story, and ask them to comment on anything that you may have brought along also. When you have finished, see how your relatives feel about staying in touch with regard to your new quest, as it may be that future research problems can also be solved with their assistance.

As soon as possible, spend a bit of time going over your notes, whilst your memory of the conversation is clear. Write or type them up, making sure you have the date of your conversation recorded, and then see if anything can be added to your rough tree drawing. Remember that at this stage, you have not necessarily been recording fact, you have been recording memory, and it is not always the same thing. Despite this, no matter how ludicrous, inaccurate or unlikely some stories may seem, these notes are still a valuable asset for the future – not just because of the information that may help, but because of the insight that they can give to future generations about the relatives you have just interviewed.

Recording your research

Now that you are beginning to get things going, it is absolutely vital to keep a record at all times of what you are doing, who you have spoken to, what sources you have consulted, and what you still wish to look at. This will help prevent duplication of effort in the future.

There are two methods for recording your efforts. The first is the age old method of using a pen and paper, employing source sheets and family group sheets. You can create your own, buy them or download them from the internet. The columns in these sheets must allow you to adequately describe the sources you have examined, where and when they were looked at, and the key points to have emerged from them. The family group sheets will then allow you to record the extracted information from these sources for each family unit, namely each set of parents in your tree and their children. Don't try to include more than this on each sheet; for each new generation start a new one.

The second method is to compile a family tree using a computer or internet based recording programme. The advantage with using a computer is that as well as giving you options to record both sources and family groupings, you can also manipulate the information in different ways once it has been input. At the click of a button, a family group sheet can be converted into a family tree diagram, for example. On the down side, if your computer fails, or a website ceases to function, you may lose everything; it is therefore *vital* to constantly back up your findings.

The following are some of the better known programmes available to purchase:

Family Historian (PC)	**www.family-historian.co.uk**
Family Tree Maker (PC)	**www.familytreemaker.com**
Legacy Family Tree (PC)	**www.legacyfamilytree.com**
Roots Magic (PC)	**www.rootsmagic.co.uk**
Reunion (Mac)	**www.leisterpro.com**
Heredis (Mac)	**www.myheredis.com**

With the exception of Family Tree Maker, most offer a basic trial version which can be downloaded from the website, usually for thirty days, which will allow you to experiment before you buy.

Sources Summary Sheet

Husband				Wife		
Researched by						
Date	Name of source	Repository and/or source number	Type of Info	Information Found		Follow up / to do

Family Group Sheet

Prepared by				Relationship to Preparer			
Address				Date			
HUSBAND		Occupation			Religion		
	Day Month Year		Town/City	County	State or Country		
Born							
Christened							Church
Married							Church
Died							Cause
Buried							Cemetery
Father			Previous spouse		Will		
Mother							
WIFE		Occupation			Religion		
Born							
Christened							Church
Married							Church
Died							Cause
Buried							Cemetery
Father			Previous spouse		Will		
Mother							

	Sex	Children	Birth		Birthplace		Date/Place of Marriage	Date of Death/Cause
	M/F/U		Day Month Year	Town/City	County	State or Country	Name of Spouse	Place
1								
2								
3								
4								
5								

Source sheets and family group sheets will help you to keep on top of your research.

A completely free programme called *Personal Ancestral File* can be downloaded from the FamilySearch website at **www.familysearch.org**, along with its sister programme PAF Charting Companion. Both are popularly used, but more restrictive. The Charting Companion site allows you to print a narrow range of charts, only to three generations, but can be updated to the professional version

Family Historian is one of the better software programmes on the market.

for just $6.75. A much better programme that can be freely downloaded is *Family Tree Builder*, available at **www.myheritage.com/family-tree-builder**. You can also choose to save your tree on an online site, with the following amongst those available for free:

Geni.com	**www.geni.com**
Ancestry	**www.ancestry.co.uk**
Tribal Pages	**www.tribalpages.com**
Genes Reunited	**www.genesreunited.com**

Having established the method by which you wish to start recording your family history, it is now time to get started with some research into the records.

Tip: Why?

At times you may come across information that on the face of it may seem really uninteresting, but always keep asking questions of yourself with every discovery you make. Your ancestor may have been an agricultural labourer, for example – but what did that actually mean, what did he physically do for a living, where did he do it, why did he seemingly keep moving house once a year, what was the local area like, who were the landlords, etc? Question everything until you run out of questions!

Further Reading

SHROMPTON, Jayne (2008) *Family Photographs and How to Date Them*. Newbury: Countryside Books.

2. *Knowing where to look*

There are many different archives and records repositories which can help with your family tree research. The major archives are based in Edinburgh, but there are also significant libraries and resources throughout the country. It is therefore useful to understand the lay of the land, to point out some of the most important archives and where to find them.

The ScotlandsPeople Centre

ScotlandsPeople Centre, HM General Register House, 2 Princes Street, Edinburgh EH1 3YY
Tel: (0131) 314 4300
[w] **www.scotlandspeoplehub.gov.uk**

The ScotlandsPeople Centre is the main port of call for genealogical research in Scotland, containing records from three key institutions – the General Register Office for Scotland (GROS), the Court of the Lord Lyon, and the National Archives of Scotland (NAS).

Access is gained to the centre through the main entrance of HM General Register House located at the east end of Princes Street (behind the mounted statue of the Duke of Wellington, and across the road from both the Balmoral Hotel and Edinburgh Waverley train station). If it is your first visit, you can do a free two hour 'taster' session, from 10.00am – 12.00pm or 2.00 to 4.00pm, which will introduce you to the basic computer system. These sessions are held in the Adam Dome, and cannot be booked in advance, so just turn up and be seated! Alternatively, for a full day's session from 9.00am to 4.30pm, a pass costing £10 will facilitate unlimited access to the records for the whole day. For this you will usually be seated in the Matheson Dome or the Reid Room, and it is always wise to book a seat in advance by telephone. The Dundas Room in New Register House is another research room, primarily reserved for professional genealogists, though the library there is accessible to all.

If you require help with your research, an assisted research service is also available for up to two hours (at a rate of £20 per hour), whereby a member of the staff can help with your queries.

The aim of the ScotlandsPeople Centre is to provide easy access, at a single terminal, to the most commonly used digitised records from each of the three component institutions. The system allows you to view the following:

Statutory births, marriages and deaths from 1855 to the present day
Church of Scotland old parochial registers (OPRs) from 1553 to 1854
The Scottish Census from 1841 to 1901
Wills and testaments from 1500 to 1901
Heraldic records from 1627 to 1909 (at time of writing – updated each year by a year)

The ScotlandsPeople Centre on Edinburgh's Princes Street.

All of these will be dealt with in much further detail in later chapters. It should be noted that these key records can also be consulted online at the ScotlandsPeople website at **www.scotlandspeople.gov.uk**, though there are some restrictions to the statutory birth, marriage and death records available through this site. Birth entries for the last 100 years cannot be viewed online, nor marriage records for the last 75 years, or deaths for the last 50 years. Indexes for births and deaths are available online to the present day, however, and official extracts can then be ordered up either from the GROS (prices are listed at **www.gro-scotland.gov.uk/files2/family-records/leaflet-s2.pdf**) or at the centre. Ordering in person at the centre, with the correct document reference number to hand, is the cheapest way to obtain these extracts.

In addition, the centre holds many other useful sources, and its computers can also be used to access a collection of externally based website resources during your research. A useful example would be if you were to discover a soldier in your family who died fighting during the First World War. A death certificate will provide the soldier's basic details such as name, service number, regiment and date and place of death. However, Ancestry (**www.ancestry.co.uk**) might provide you with his full service record if it has survived, as well as a medal index card, the NAS catalogue (see below) will allow you to look for a will which may have been registered whilst he was on active service, the Commonwealth War Graves Commission website (**www.cwgc.org**) can help to identify where he was buried, and other sites such as FindmyPast (**www.findmy**

past.co.uk) may provide access to an entry within the *Soldiers Who Died in the Great War* collection, which might include additional information such as a birthplace.

The standard birth, marriage, death, census and parish register records are also backed up on microfilm and microfiche, which sometimes need to be viewed for the occasional record which may have been poorly digitised. The 1851 census is a good example, where many entries which were recorded on blue paper in blue ink did not scan too well. Some additional materials exist only on microfilm or fiche, such as a limited collection of kirk session material, OPR death records and some monumental inscriptions, many of which also exist in book form within the site's extensive library located in the Dundas Room. This can be consulted by all visitors, no matter which room you are seated within, and additional works of use for your research include university alumni lists, records of church ministers from various denominations, and more – the catalogue is at **www.scotlandspeoplehub.gov.uk/research/library. html**. There are also holdings in an e-library, listed at **www.scotlandspeoplehub.gov.uk/research/ e-library.html**, which can only be accessed at the centre.

Visiting the centre

Upon arrival, you will be guided from the shop area to the main desk at the Adam Dome, where you will be based if you have come to do a two hour taster session. It is worth noting that if you bring a laptop, you will have to run it off battery in here (mains power is available elsewhere in the centre). If you have come to the centre for the day, you will be steered towards the room where your seat is located, and where you will pay your admission fee at the supervisors' desk.

Once seated, on a first visit you will need to register your details on the computer to which you have been allocated in order to create a personalised account, with a username (based on your name) and a temporary password. After logging in you can then set a permanent password of your choice and register fully with your name, address, and e-mail details. Before you get started with your research, make sure that your mobile phone is switched off!

On the left hand side of the screen are links to the digitised records collections, which can take you to a dedicated search screen into which you can type the details of your request. After inputting your search terms, clicking 'Search' then brings up a further screen with the results for that enquiry, and an option to then see the original digitised image for the desired record. 'Wildcards', which can help if you don't know the exact spelling of a name, can be used within searches, as can the 'Soundex' system of name variants, which allows you to check for surnames by alternative written forms based on how they sound. A help icon at the end of each search field is there to help if you are unclear about what to do.

Entries can be printed from the onscreen records, and to do this you will need to provide credit on your account in advance at the supervisor's desk. There are some restrictions however – births less than a hundred years old, marriages less than seventy five and deaths less than fifty years old cannot be printed out, and must be ordered as formal extracts at a cost of £8 per record. At the end of your session, unused credit can

The ScotlandsPeople Centre computer system.

be carried over for a future visit, or refunded. There are a series of printers in each room from which you can print and collect your copies, and records can also be saved onto a USB memory stick. The various costs involved for this can be viewed online at **www.scotlandspeoplehub.gov.uk.**

Tip: Opening hours

Always check the website prior to a visit to make sure that the centre is open on the day on which you wish to visit. Scotland traditionally enjoys regional bank holidays, such as the fairs in Glasgow and Edinburgh which are held on separate dates in July, so you may find that whilst some institutions are open in parts of Scotland on a particular date, they could well be closed elsewhere on the same day.

Strathclyde Area Genealogy Centre

22 Park Circus, Glasgow, G3 6BE
Tel: 0141 287 8364   [w] **www.glasgow.gov.uk/en/Residents/BirthDeathMarriage_Citizenship/GenealogyCentre**

The Strathclyde Area Genealogy Centre provides unlimited access to the digitised images of Scotland's birth, marriage and death records, both before and after statutory registration, as well as census images, for a flat out daily fee of £14. Unlike the ScotlandsPeople Centre, the site only has microfiche back ups for events recorded in the Strathclyde area, and from 1855 to 1993 only, though the online images cover the whole of Scotland to the present day. The centre also has pre-1855 OPR microfilms for the Strathclyde area.

The National Archives of Scotland (NAS)

The National Archives of Scotland, HM General Register House, 2 Princes Street, Edinburgh EH1 3YY
Tel: 0131 535 1314 [w] **www.nas.gov.uk**

The National Archives of Scotland is the main repository for archived records in the country, with search rooms based at two main buildings in Edinburgh, at HM General Register House on Princes Street, and at West Register House on Charlotte Square, each of which deals with specific sets of records. Whichever building you wish to visit, on your first trip you will need to bring two passport sized photographs with you, and two forms of identification, in order to gain a reader's ticket.

Prior to any visit, it is worth consulting the archive's online catalogue at **www.nas.gov.uk/onlinecatalogue**. This allows you to do a search by keywords (for example, for a family member or institution), by reference number and by year. If an item is listed, it is worth calling in advance to check that it will be available when you plan to visit, and at which building it is held. In some cases the required documents may be held at an outside storage facility and you may need to order them well in advance to allow time for their delivery.

Some material can be photocopied or photographed by the NAS on your behalf, depending on its condition, but digital photography is not allowed.

(i) General Register House

Whilst the ScotlandsPeople Centre is mostly based on the ground floor of General Register House, the NAS's own dedicated search rooms are located upstairs, but access to these is gained via the garden entrance at the rear of the building, which has the words 'Sasine Office' marked in stone above the door. You will be asked to leave your coat and bag in the locker room (remember to bring some change!), and to then carry anything you wish to use in the search rooms in a clear plastic bag, which will be supplied. Laptops can be used in the search rooms, but if you wish to take written notes, you will need to do so with a pencil.

Once ready, walk up the stairs and make your way through the Legal Search Room, where you will see lots of professional solicitors and commercial researchers investigating land records and other public registers. You will soon come to an information desk, and if you are unsure of what records you require to see, the staff here will provide some friendly guidance. At this reception area there are various indexes to the NAS holdings on surrounding shelves, and some other records such as wills calendars (books recording summaries of confirmed wills and inventories), indexes to the Registers of Deeds, and other materials which you will most likely find yourself using from time to time. If you require records on microfilm or fiche, the staff will show you where to access and view them.

The main location for your research, however, will be the magnificent oak panelled Historical Search Room, to which you will be guided. It is in here that you can consult church records, legal registers and property records, some court records, estate papers, wills and testaments, burgh records, state papers, and much more. You will need to hand your reader's ticket to the archivist at the main service desk, who will then allocate you a seat and table.

At one end of the room is a series of computers on which you can locate the digitised holdings of the NAS, whilst other tables in the room can be used to consult original records. Be advised that if a particular record has been digitised, such as a kirk session book, you will not be allowed to view the original. There are also two computer terminals in the room for the exclusive use of those wishing to order up original records using the archive's catalogue and internal ordering system.

It should go without saying, but if you are planning to view original materials, make sure that your hands are clean before starting. For the more precious materials white gloves can be provided as well sets of cushions and weights to hold documents down, many of which are printed on sturdy papers and parchments, and which can be difficult to make lie flat. If you have problems trying to open a particular document, ask one of the archivists to help rather than apply some of your own tender loving aggression!

Access to the National Archives of Scotland is via the old Sasine Office entrance behind the ScotlandsPeople Centre.

(ii) West Register House

West Register House is the second of the NAS buildings open to the public, within which you can view court and government records, maps, plans, and some additional digitised materials also available at General Register House.

The building is located at Charlotte Square, off the west end of Princes Street, and operates in a similar way to General Register House. As before, you will be asked to leave your belongings in a locker and to transfer any materials you need into a clear bag, after which you can proceed up the stairs to the West Search Room. If your visit to the building is a first at any NAS property, you will again be asked to register before being allocated a seat, though if you have previously registered at General Register House, the same reader's ticket will be valid. Once you have gained a seat, you can then order up materials using the same computer system as described earlier, with the terminals located at the rear of the room.

Unlike General Register House, which has the ScotlandsPeople café next door, West Register House has no catering facilities at all. The nearest place to find some lunch is therefore on Princes Street, a couple of minutes walk away.

National Library of Scotland (NLS)
George IV Bridge, Edinburgh, EH1 1EW
Tel: 0131 623 3700   Fax: 0131 623 3701 [w] **www.nls.uk**

The National Library of Scotland is a wonderful resource carrying a great deal of genealogically useful material, including electoral rolls, newspapers, maps, records of emigration (published and unpublished), state papers, family histories and estate archives, directories (street, trade, military, ecclesiastical, peerages, etc), and more. Of note is the library's India Papers Collection (**www.nls.uk/family-history/india-papers/index.htm**), the largest collection in the UK outside of the British Library in London, containing some four thousand volumes of material relating to Britain's presence in the country. The institution's main catalogue is well worth bookmarking at **http://main-cat.nls. uk/cgi-bin/Pwebrecon.cgi?DB=local&PAGE=First.**

The library offers two types of reader's ticket, the first being a short term ticket valid for four weeks, the second a general reader's ticket valid for three years. Proof of identity in the form of a document carrying your name and address, and your signature or photograph is required, though the library will accept personal ID with a utilities document carrying details of your present address, such as a phone bill.

With a reader's ticket, you can not only visit the premises in Edinburgh, you can also access some material from home, such as the online version of the Oxford Dictionary of National Biography. The library also has many other useful online collections that do not require a ticket, such as its extensive maps collection (**www.nls.uk/family-history/maps/index.html**). At Hillington in Renfrewshire, access can be provided to thousands of films held within the Scottish Screen Archive (**www.nls.uk/ssa/index.html**), which became a part of the NLS in 2007. Many of these films can be previewed online.

The facility also hosts many exhibitions and events by keynote speakers at its George IV Bridge Building, which can be booked online at **www.nls.uk/events/index.html** or by calling (0131) 623 3918.

Regional archives

If the records that you need to find are not held at the NAS, you can also try the local county records office for your area. Even if you can find relevant material at the NAS, the local archive is still worth consulting for any additional documents.

Some years ago, I discovered that my three times great grandmother had been murdered in 1866 at a farm in Perthshire. Beyond finding a death certificate there were two obvious starting points for my research into this. The first was to find any newspaper coverage of the event, the second to find if anybody had been prosecuted for it. The A. K. Bell Library in Perth had microfilms of several relevant local newspapers, and the NAS did indeed turn out to have trial papers, though the accused was eventually found non-proven. However, I also approached the Perth and Kinross Archives to see if they might have anything else on the case. They came up trumps, with a series of letters written by the police throughout the investigation describing various arrests and other developments. In addition, they also had many other police records from the time that showed just how stretched the Perthshire County Constabulary was as a force, with another murder enquiry on the go and a major cattle plague epidemic in the county to contend with, which provided some useful additional context.

The Scottish Archive Network (SCAN) provides an online catalogue to the holdings of most county re-cords offices at **www. scan.org. uk/ catalogue**. It works very similarly to the NAS catalogue, and in performing a search, you can locate where a record might exist, a description of it, and whether it is accessible. Some local archives also have their own online search systems.

A list of local archives operating in Scotland is located at Appendix 1.

The SCAN catalogue can helpfully locate records within county archives.

Family History Centres

There are an increasing number of dedicated family history centres being set up by local authorities across Scotland, such as the Burns Monument Centre at Kilmarnock (**www.burnsmonumentcentre.com**) which opened in March 2009. These can provide regional access to the digitised records of the ScotlandsPeople Centre, as well as many local resources. Where the digitised records of the GROS are available, there will be a fee, but other records will be free to access, such as newspaper collections and micro-films of poor relief, census and parish records.

LDS Family History Centres

[w] **www.familysearch.org**

The Church of Jesus Christ of Latter-Day Saints, known more commonly as the Mormon Church, is a worldwide Christian religion with a membership of 13 million adherents. With its headquarters in Salt Lake City, Utah, the Church has a theological requirement for its members to research their family histories, and as such has provided many different research aids to help its members and others in this task.

Many original Scottish records, in addition to compiled family trees by its members, can be consulted at its network of local family history centres, of which there are 16 within Scotland. Chapter 5 discusses both these records and the family history centres in more detail.

Family History Societies

Throughout Scotland there exists a network of local family history societies, ranging from large established groups such as the Glasgow and West of Scotland FHS and Aberdeen and North East Scotland FHS to relative newcomers such as Moray & Nairn FHS established in 2009. These societies are a great way to seek help from others in your locality who may well be researching the same families, areas or records as yourself. Whilst each society is completely independent, the majority subscribe to an umbrella body called the Scottish Association of Family History Societies (**www.safhs.org.uk**).

The individual groups charge a basic annual subscription fee (some also offer family subscriptions), in return for which you will receive a regular series of journals which carry a range of useful articles as well as adverts for those trying to establish connections with other members. There is also free admission to a monthly series of lectures, which will explore a range of interesting historical subjects and records types of genealogical interest. Whilst some of the larger organisations have their own premises and research centres, smaller groups such as Largs and North Ayrshire FHS tend to meet at the local library on a monthly basis, with more limited resources available.

Family history societies are also a great forum where you can contribute research via a series of locally run projects, the most useful of which are perhaps the monumental inscriptions recording projects that are undertaken in local kirkyards across the length and breadth of Scotland. A list of all known societies is located at Appendix 2.

Tip: Keep up to date!

The various institutions dealing with items of interest to those researching their Scottish genealogy are constantly announcing new records releases, exhibitions and acquisitions. A useful way to keep up to date with all the different developments is to subscribe to a family history publication. Most directly useful for Scottish research is Discover my Past Scotland magazine (www.discovermypast.co.uk), but many British magazines regularly also include Scottish material, including Your Family Tree (www.yourfamilytreemag.co.uk), Ancestors (www.ancestorsmagazine.co.uk), Practical Family History (www.familytree.co.uk) and Family History Monthly (www.familyhistorymonthly.com).

For more instant developments, my own free to access Scottish Genealogy News and Events blog (www.scottishancestry.blogspot.com) is just one of many sources providing up to date news, with others including Eastman's Online Genealogy Newsletter (http://blog.eogn.com), Dear Myrtle (http://blog.dearmyrtle.com) and Anglo-Celtic Connections (http://anglo-celtic-connections.blogspot.com).

Above: The Scottish Association of Family History Societies website can point you to your nearest FHS.
Left: Keep up to date with the genealogical world with magazines such as Discover My Past Scotland.

The Scottish Genealogy Society

15 Victoria Terrace, Edinburgh, EH1 2JL
Tel/Fax: 0131 220 3677
[w] **www.scotsgenealogy.com**

Founded in 1953, and based in Edinburgh, the Scottish Genealogy Society holds an extensive collection of books, microfilms and fiche within its library, as well as many privately gifted family histories and records collections deposited by its members over the years. It also offers a regular series of monthly lectures and produces a quarterly journal entitled *The Scottish Genealogist*.

The society's website holds a Family History Index detailing some of the private family history papers held within its library, which can be consulted on site or ordered as copies through its photocopying service. There are also many useful research guides online, covering a wide range of subjects, and a shop. In particular the site has a useful discussion forum, open to members and non-members alike, at **www.yabbers.com/phpbb/scotsgen.html**.

The National Archives (TNA)

The National Archives, Kew, Richmond, Surrey, TW9 4DU

[w] **www.nationalarchives.gov.uk**

As part of the United Kingdom, a great deal of material for Scotland can also be sourced from the National Archives in England, including records as diverse as military papers and apprenticeship taxes. The archive has an ongoing digitisation programme of records, many of which can be accessed through its own Documents Online service at **www.nationalarchives.gov.uk/documentsonline**, though the facility also collaborates on many projects with partner organisations such as FindmyPast and Ancestry.

Unlike the NAS, it is possible to photograph original documents within the reading rooms at Kew, so long as a flash is not used.

The Society of Genealogists

Society of Genealogists, 14 Charterhouse Buildings, Goswell Road, London, EC1M 7BA

Tel: (020) 7251 8799   Fax: (020) 7250 1800   [w] **www.sog.org.uk**

Located in London, the Society of Genealogists hosts a research library occupying three separate floors, which contains a great deal of Scottish material, including copies on microfilm of Scottish statutory and church vital events records. The society also regularly offers talks on various subjects of interest to the Scottish genealogist. An online catalogue of its holdings, known as SOGCAT, is available at **http://62.32.98.6/S10312UK-Staff/OPAC/index.asp**.

Tip:

Many records remain in private hands or in other repositories across Britain. Three useful online catalogues to help you to locate these, if they have been registered with an archive, are the National Register of Archives for Scotland at www.nas.gov.uk/onlineregister and the English based National Register of Archives at www.nationalarchives.gov.uk/nra/default.asp. The Access to Archives site at www.nationalarchives.gov.uk/a2a can also help you to locate Scottish material held within English and Welsh archives.

The Guild of One Name Studies

Tel: 0800 011 2182   [w] **www.one-name.org**

The Guild of One Names Studies, affectionately known as the 'GOONS', is a body of dedicated volunteers who have each undertaken to study a single surname in records from across the English speaking world. Membership of the Guild costs £15 annually and entitles members to a range of benefits. Newcomers are first provided with a Members' Handbook, which offers tips and advice on projects and the workings of the society itself, and they are also issued with their own Guild e-mail address. Access is further granted to the private area of the group's website, which contains additional resources not available to the general public, including the Guild Knowledge Store and research made available online by fellow researchers. In addition, the society issues the professionally produced Journal of One Name Studies four times a year.

A condition of registering a one-name study with the Guild is that members are obliged to answer any queries from the general public. If you have a particular problem, therefore, with a person bearing a rare surname in your tree, and that surname is being studied by a Guild member, you may potentially be able to save yourself a small fortune by e-mailing that member for some help. Many guild members also run their own DNA surname projects, using Y-chromosome DNA tests to chart the spread of a surname and to see which branches of a family may be related to each other (see Chapter 10). A list of over 2000 surnames currently being studied by the Guild is available at **www.one-name.org/register.html**.

The Union

Scotland was for many centuries a politically independent country, until the Stuart king James VI acceded to the throne of England in 1603, becoming James I of Great Britain. During his rule the foundations for the British Empire were cemented, with the colonies founded in Ulster and America amongst the king's imperial achievements. As an independent country from England, however, Scotland harboured its own ambitions as a nation, and in 1698 threw much of its resources into an expedition to establish a colony at the bay of Darien in the Isthmus of Panama. The first five ships sailed from Leith in July with 1200 people aboard, arriving in Panama in early November. So disastrous was the venture that it was abandoned in July 1699. A second fleet set sail in November 1699, equally doomed to disaster, with most of the 2500 colonists perishing soon after.

With Scotland's nobles virtually bankrupted, full political union between the two countries followed in 1707, much to the dismay of the general public, during the reign of Queen Anne, the last ruler of a Stuart dynasty which had held power in Scotland for centuries. A strong sense of national identity was maintained, however, through the preservation of the country's very separate legal and education systems, as well as its own state religion. Opposition to the Union was initially strong, and the Jacobite rebellions of 1715, 1719 and 1745 were partly fuelled by anti-Union sentiment, but these were crushed by the Hanoverian dynasty which had come to power in Britain following the death of Anne in 1714.

In 1999, after many years of campaigning, Scotland finally regained its own parliament.

3. *Statutory records*

The most useful documents to start with when constructing a family tree are the statutory records of Scottish births, marriages and deaths, the registration of which commenced on January 1st 1855. The most comprehensive online source for these is the ScotlandsPeople website, with the records also viewable at the ScotlandsPeople Centre in Edinburgh and at other family history centres across the country. The register entries contain considerably more information than their equivalents in England, Wales and Ireland, making it much easier to establish connections between the generations.

The early registers were actually deposited at the GROS each year, with copies retained by the local district registrars. This means that in the birth and death entries at the GROS, you will find the original signatures of informants, though not in marriage entries, where the records were compiled by the registrar from information supplied in marriage schedules, which had to be filled out prior to a wedding taking place. Today the records are transmitted by the local registrars to Edinburgh electronically.

From time to time, the information required by the registrars was revised, and so the records do not provide the same levels of detail consistently. In 1855, they were clearly very keen, with birth records recorded across two pages of the registration book. By the end of the year, writer's cramp appears to have set in, and from 1856 the records were simplified considerably, with a further revision from 1861 producing the basic formula that would remain largely unchanged to the present day.

One thing to remember when searching for an entry in the statutory records is that the registrar will have recorded names under the spelling that he or she will have deemed to be correct. A MacDonald may be listed as a McDonald in the register, or a Smyth as a Smith. A good example lies with a death I once located in Airdrie from 1861. An Irish born railway stoker called John Brogan had died at the age of 34, with his father listed as **Yohan Brogan**. In other records, this same father was also noted as **Owen** and **John**. In fact, his baptismal name was **Eoin**, which is the Irish Gaelic equivalent of John, and pronounced as 'Yohan'. Clearly for some time he had tried to use his Gaelic name in Scotland, and the confused registrars listed him as they saw fit!

Tip: Tracing Descendants
Tracing forwards with your family history can often be as useful as researching back. Siblings of your ancestor may have inherited documents, family bibles and other material which they may then have passed on to their descendants. Locating your cousins may therefore be as profitable as researching your forebears, and can be done with the same records used to trace your ancestors.

Births

Page 16.

18_64_. BIRTHS in the *Parish* of *Blackford* in the *County* of *Perth*

No.	Name and Surname.	When and Where Born.	Sex.	Name, Surname, & Rank or Profession of Father. Name, and Maiden Surname of Mother. Date and Place of Marriage.	Signature and Qualification of Informant, and Residence, if out of the House in which the Birth occurred.	When and Where Registered, and Signature of Registrar.
46	John McKeith	1864. August Tenth 5h. 10m. A.M. Loan Tullibardine	M.	John McKeith Railway Labourer Helen McKeith M.S. Lauder 1859. February 18th at Tullibardine	Donie Lauder Grandfather and Occupier residing at Blackford Loan of Tullibardine	1864. August 19th At Blackford John Miller Registrar
47	David Hepburn Paton	1864. August Fifteenth 4h. 45m. P.M. New Street Blackford	M.	William Hay Paton Currier Janet Paton M.S. Rodger 1859. December 2d Parish of Kincleaven	William Hay Paton Father not Present	1864. August 25th At Blackford John Miller Registrar
48	James Kelly	1864. August Eighteenth 11h. 30m. P.M. Muirhead Kincardine	M.	James Kelly Ploughman Susan Kelly M.S. McNamara 1858. January 30th Milton Malbay Ireland	James Kelly Father not Present	1864 September 3d at Blackford John Miller Registrar

John Miller Registrar

The birth entry for my great grandfather, David Hepburn Paton.

Birth certificates from 1856 will contain the following:
- Name of child (and whether illegitimate)
- Where born (street, number and parish), and at what date and time
- The sex of the child
- The father's name and occupation
- The mother's name, including maiden surname and any previous married surnames
- The date and location of the parents' marriage
- The name of the informant, residence if not at the place of birth, and whether present at the event
- The date and place of registration, and the registrar's name

For births between 1856 and 1860, the registrars unfortunately did not record the marriage details for the parents, though this was restored in 1861. If, however, you find that your ancestor was born in 1855, then you are in for a treat, as the records contain the following additional information:
- The father's age and birthplace
- The number of children produced by the parents, and how many still alive
- The mother's age and birthplace

Leaving 1855 aside, the key significant differences to similar registration documents elsewhere in the United Kingdom are the provision of a date and location for the parents' marriage, and the mother's maiden name.

A good example of how this might help lies with Irish ancestors who settled in Scotland. Most census returns will simply list 'Ireland' as a birthplace for these immigrants, making it difficult to locate where they originally came from. The statutory registration of Roman Catholic marriages in Ireland did not commence until 1864, and so if your ancestors left the country and subsequently had children born in Scotland from 1855 onwards, their place and date of marriage in Ireland might be listed, providing you with the necessary details to take your search further back on the Emerald Isle. If your male ancestor had a fairly common name like O' Neill, the fact that his wife is listed with her maiden name will also make it much more likely that the correct marriage can be effectively traced.

If a child was born illegitimately, this fact will be recorded under its name in the first column of the record. Usually he or she will be recorded with the mother's surname, though if the father was present, the couple could request it to be registered under his name also, with the father then also signing the document as an informant. If the father was not present, he could not be recorded in the entry. In Scotland, an illegitimate child automatically became legitimate if his parents subsequently married. If this was the case, there may be a note in the margin attesting to the fact. You may also find in such a case that a person's birth has in fact been re-recorded many years later in the main register, under the father's surname, when the parents wished it to be explicitly recorded that the child was no longer to be known by the mother's maiden name, or any other name.

In addition to the ScotlandsPeople website, an index to Scottish statutory births from 1855 to 1875 can be found on the International Genealogical Index (see Chapter 5).

Tip:
When looking for a birth, don't necessarily assume that the child will pop up nine months after the parents' wedding day – the mother may well have been heavily pregnant and anxious to make sure that the child's birth was legitimate, or may have already had children illegitimately prior to the wedding day.

Unusual Surnames

We usually think of people having a Christian name and surname as a standard and sometimes a middle name, particularly from the mid 19th century onwards. However, there were other ways that people in Scotland could be named, particularly in areas where many people may have shared the same surnames within a small community. In the north east of Scotland, including Shetland and Orkney, many people in small communities adopted what was known as a 'tee name'. This was a form of nickname, often derived by joining a forename to a mother's forename, such as Georgie-Mary, or by some other attribute, such as an occupation, e.g. Noble-Farmer, with that person's descendants also inheriting the 'Farmer' tee name. In census returns these 'tee names' are often recorded as the surname, and the real surname may confusingly appear as an initial only, e.g. John N. Farmer. A fascinating article by Stuart Mitchell on a similar phenomenon of people using surname aliases in Upper Banffshire in the 18th Century is online at http://tinyurl.com/o947jo.

In Gaelic speaking communities there was a similar situation, with the population of a small island only able to distinguish between so many John MacLeods, for example! In such a case, a particular John MacLeod may well have been known more colloquially in Gaelic by a nickname to help identify him more easily, such as 'Iain Dubh', or 'dark-haired John'. This may have been subsequently recorded in documents by non-Gaelic speakers as 'John Duff'.

Marriages

In Scotland, there were various ways that one could be wed, which will be dealt with more fully in Chapter 4. Some people lived as if they were married, without having actually gone through any formal ceremony, a practice known as 'living by cohabitation and repute'. If challenged they simply had to provide evidence of living together as man and wife. As the welfare state developed, most people did in fact register these 'irregular' marriages. In some cases however, you may find a man referring to his wife, perhaps in a will, but then find no marriage record in the register, or one which has been registered many years after the couple first got together.

Marriage registers from 1856 will contain the following information:
- Date and location of marriage
- Whether a civil or religious ceremony
- Groom's name, signature, occupation, status (bachelor or widower), age and residence
- Status of groom's parents (whether deceased); mother's maiden name and additional married names if remarried; father's occupation
- Bride's name, signature, occupation (spinster or widow), age and residence
- Officiating minister or whether by authority of a warrant
- Witnesses names (and for later entries addresses)
- Date and place of registration

In addition, for the year 1855 only, the records contained the following additional details:
- Birthplace of each partner
- Number of previous marriages for each partner
- The number of children produced from those marriages

The birthplace of an individual was eventually restored to the certificates from 1972 onwards. If the bride or groom could not write, an X will have been written instead, with the signature of the registrar noted beside it as verification that it was marked in his or her presence.

As with births, an index to Scottish statutory marriages from 1855 to 1875 can be found online at the International Genealogical Index (see Chapter 5). Another source which may be of some limited assistance is the UK Marriage Witness Index 1655-1992 database, located at **www.worldvitalrecords.com**. This collection of records is small, with just 58,816 names from across the UK, though there are many Scottish entries. Unlike ScotlandsPeople and the IGI, it can be usefully searched for the names of witnesses who attended the weddings noted, as well as for the contracting parties.

> *Tips: Stray Scots*
> *If you have a Scottish ancestor who you think may have moved to England, it is worth checking the Manchester and Lancashire FHS website at www.mlfhs.org.uk. The Anglo-Scottish branch page on the site hosts a list of marriages which took place in the country, where at least one of the parties contracting to be married was Scottish, helpfully listing where in Scotland he or she was originally from.*

Death records

All death events registered in Scotland from 1855 will contain the following information:

- The name of the deceased
- Date of death, time, and location (with usual residence also recorded if not the same)
- Marital status, and name of spouse
- Name of deceased's father, occupation, and whether alive or deceased
- Name of deceased's mother, with maiden surname, and whether alive or deceased
- The cause of death, and person certifying the death
- Informant, and relationship to the deceased

Down the years, the details recorded have again varied. In 1855, the registrar also noted the following extra details:

- The names of any children born to the deceased, their ages, and if they were deceased before 1855, their date of death.
- The place of the deceased's burial and the name of the undertaker responsible

From 1856 onwards, the information on children was removed, though the burial information remained in the records until 1860. On the down side, the name of a spouse from 1856 to 1860 disappeared temporarily. From 1967, the deceased's date of birth has very helpfully been recorded.

Some of the illnesses described in early death records can seem incredibly unfamiliar. Tuberculosis, a major problem in 19th and early 20th century Britain was previously known by many names, including 'phthisis pulmonala', 'consumption', and 'decline'. Epidemics were also prevalent in the recent past – in Glasgow, the Daily News recorded eleven instances of bubonic plague as recently as September 1900, whilst in 1918, the H1N1 virus, aka 'Spanish Flu', killed more people than during the whole of the First World War. Websites such as **www.medterms.com/script/main/hp.asp** can help to explain some of the ailments that you may encounter.

Tip: Statutory Registration
The Scottish Way of Birth and Death website at www.gla.ac.uk/departments/ scottishwayofbirthanddeath, from the University of Glasgow's Centre for the History of Medicine, is a fantastic resource explaining the history of Scottish statutory registration from 1855 to 1939. Produced in conjunction with the Wellcome Trust, it details the efforts to get the system up and running, and also provides a useful insight into how registration was of benefit to determining medical policy within the country.

Additional birth, marriage and death registers
There are various other birth, marriage and death registers held by the GROS, which have been digitised and made available to view as part of the main record collections at the ScotlandsPeople Centre and website. These include marine registers for births and deaths from 1855, which recorded any child born to a Scottish father or the death of any Scottish subject at sea; registers of births, marriages and deaths from 1860 to 1965 for children born to Scottish parents, or of Scots who married or died abroad; and the High Commissioners' returns for births, marriages and death from 1964 for those living in countries belonging to the Commonwealth. From 1881 there have also been registers for all three events for families involved in the army, and from April 1959 for all three armed forces, whilst air registers were established in 1948 for births and deaths in airplanes. In addition there have been specific registers for military deaths occurring during the South African War of 1899-1902, the First World War from 1914-1918, and the Second World War from 1939-1945.

In February 2009, the Book of Scottish Connections was also established, allowing people living overseas with a Scottish family link to register an overseas event with the GROS for a fee, whether that be a birth, marriage, civil partnership or death, as long as it has been previously registered in the country where the event occurred. A certificate is issued in return. Applications can be made online at www.gro-scotland.gov.uk/regscot/book-of-scottish-connections.html.

Other statutory records which can be consulted at the ScotlandsPeople Centre include:

Register of Corrected Entries

If an event needed to be amended after an initial registration, the correction will have been made in the *Register of Corrected Entries*, and a note placed in the margin of the original record. You may find, for example, that a child's name might be amended after a christening, the parents having had a change of heart, and any time there was a suspicious or unusual death registered, it was usually referred to the procurator fiscal to investigate the circumstances, with a summary of the verdict included in an RCE entry. On the ScotlandsPeople website, a record with an attached RCE record will allow you to view this record for an additional 2 credits. The Register cannot be searched as a database in its own right.

Divorce

The *Register of Divorces* records all divorces from February 1st 1984 to the present day, providing a brief summary of final decrees, any costs incurred by the parties involved, and in some cases the names of any children born to the couple.

From 1830 to 1984, the responsibility for granting a divorce lay with the Court of Session, which had in turn taken over the responsibility from the Commissary Court of Edinburgh in 1563. As such, all records of divorce from 1563 are indexed on the online catalogue of the National Archives of Scotland, and the original records can be consulted at the centre. A useful guide to divorce can be found on the NAS website at **www.nas.gov.uk/guides/divorce.asp**.

Civil Partnerships

A *Register of Civil Partnerships* has been kept in Scotland since December 5th 2005, recording so-called 'same sex marriages' registered within the country. There is also a *Register of Dissolutions of Civil Partnership* from the same date.

Adoption

A *Register of Adoptions* was started in 1930, which records adoptions after an order has been granted by the Scottish Courts. If you were adopted, and if you are over 17 years of age, the GROS advises that you write to its Adoption Unit with a request to see the original birth entry under which you were registered, and include your birth name, date of birth and postal address. They will then issue you with a declaration form to fill in, and once received, the details can then be released to you. These may include further information, such as the names of either or both of your natural parents, and additional information concerning the birth itself, such as the location. There are no children listed in the register who were born before 1909.

For adopted children wishing to trace their natural parents, or for parents who wish to trace their adopted children, the GROS also advises contacting the Birthlink agency (**www.birthlink.org.uk**), which keeps a register of such interests. It can be contacted at

Birthlink, 21 Castle Street, Edinburgh, EH2 3DN, Tel: (0131) 225 6441. Another useful website offering advice on adoption matters is Adoption Search Reunion (**www.adoptionsearchreunion.org.uk**).

The Birthlink agency can help those wishing to trace their natural parents or adopted children.

Further Reading

BLACK, George F. (2004) *The Surnames of Scotland*. Edinburgh: Birlinn Ltd.
SINCLAIR, Cecil (2000) *Jock Tamson's Bairns – A History of the Records of the General Register Office for Scotland*. Edinburgh: General Register Office for Scotland

Civil Registration across the British Isles

You may find your Scottish ancestors elsewhere within the UK. Civil registration began in England and Wales on July 1st 1837, following the creation of the General Register Office by an Act of Parliament. The two countries were divided into 619 registration districts (623 from 1851), each overseen by a superintendent registrar, and further divided into sub-districts under the control of a local registrar. Copies of all births, marriages and deaths recorded locally were sent to the superintendent registrar, who would forward them to the Registrar General in London. Quarterly indexes were compiled from these up to 1983, though from 1984 the system changed to a series of annual indexes. The best online source for consulting the national indexes is at www.ancestry.co.uk, though many libraries hold copies on microfiche up to 2005. Original certificates can then be ordered from the GRO at Southport through www. direct.gov.uk/gro. Indexes for some local county registers can be consulted at www.ukbmd.org.uk.

In Ireland, civil registration commenced in 1845 with Protestant marriages, but it would not be until 1864 that births, marriages and deaths for the whole island would be recorded. Indexes to civil records for the whole island up to 1921 can be viewed through the FamilySearch website at http://pilot.familysearch.org/recordsearch/start.html#p=collectionDetails;t=searchable;c=1408347, whilst records for the south from 1922 to 1958 are also available on the site. Copies of records for pre-1922 events for the whole island can be ordered from the GRO for Ireland at Roscommon at www.groireland.ie, as well as for records for the south from 1922 to 1958. Northern Irish records from 1922 onwards can be ordered through www.groni.gov.uk.

The ScotlandsPeople Centre has a database of Northern Irish births from 1922 to 1993 held within the Dundas Room at New Register House, and also provides access to the FamilySearch indexes on the terminals in HM General Register House. It also holds microfiche copies of the English and Welsh indexes.

4. Parish Records

Prior to 1855, the records of the Church of Scotland, better known in Scotland as 'the Kirk', will contain the basic vital records for most, but not all, of your ancestors.

With the advent of civil registration, every established church parish in Scotland was legally required to deliver its registers of births and baptisms, banns and marriages and deaths and burials up to and including those for 1855 to the Registrar General, and those that were handed in can now be accessed in many ways. The ScotlandsPeople Centre in Edinburgh holds digitised copies of the originals, which can also be consulted via the ScotlandsPeople website (see Chapter 3). Digitised images can further be viewed at local family history centres such as the Strathclyde Area Genealogy Centre at Park Circus, Glasgow, whilst many local studies libraries and family history societies also have records relevant to their areas available on microfilm.

The Scottish Genealogy Society library in Edinburgh has an extensive microfilm collection for most of Scotland, whilst the records can also be ordered up for a small fee at the many family history centres run by the Church of Jesus Christ of Latter Day Saints. Various locally based transcription projects have been carried out across the country and placed online, such as that for the Argyll parishes of Bowmore, Kallarrow, and Kildalton, on the Isle of Islay, found at **http://homepages.rootsweb.ancestry.com/~steve/ islay/opr**. In addition, the FreeREG project at **www.freereg.org.uk** includes index entries for some Scottish parishes.

Ancestry.co.uk also has many records available as part of the UK Parish Records Collection. This collection includes some OPR records, and also records from other denominations, such as the Episcopal Church and the Roman Catholic Church.

There were also many dissenting faiths in Scotland, and many non-Presbyterian religions. Their records are not available at the ScotlandsPeople Centre, nor on the ScotlandsPeople website, and their locations will be discussed at the end of this chapter.

Researching the OPRs

The registers of the established church, known as the OPRs (old parish registers), were in fact required to be kept in Scotland from 1552, with the earliest surviving examples being those for the Perthshire parish of Errol in

Prior to 1855, church records are the next step for your research.

1553, seven years before the Reformation. Most registers however did not start until the 17th century and beyond, with some areas of Scotland, such as the Western Isles, not employing them until the 19th century. Due to the set up of the Kirk, you will not find duplicates of baptismal and marriage records within Bishop's Transcripts, as within England and Wales (and a small handful of Irish parishes), for the simple reason that, for the most part, there were no bishops! Therefore, the OPRs are the main source for information on these events, though some additional information concerning financial transactions around them may be recorded in the kirk session records (see below). A list of Church of Scotland parishes is located at **www.scotlandspeoplehub.gov.uk/re search/list-of-oprs.html**. Each has retrospectively been given a particular parish number, starting with Bressay on Shetland (including Burra and Quarff) as parish number 1, and working south as far as the Borders parish of Wigtown, numbered at 901.

The OPR records essentially fall into three main areas – births and baptisms, banns and marriages, and deaths and burials. The level of detail for each register in Scotland was dependant on the minister or session clerk, meaning that they vary enormously from parish to parish, and often within the same parish, as ministers came and ministers went.

It is also worth noting that some established church birth/baptismal, marriage and death records were kept in the kirk session registers, and were never submitted to the GROS, these registers being held instead at the NAS. A list of these is available at **www.scotlandspeoplehub.gov.uk/pdf/list-of-oprs-appendix1.pdf**.

Tip: 'of' and 'in'

Parish records can often seem scant in the information supplied, but clues can often be noted about somebody's status within a parish. In some records you will see a person listed as 'of' such and such a place, or 'of this parish', whilst in others, he or she may be noted as 'in' that place. 'Of' can imply ownership of a place, whilst' of this parish' usually means 'from this parish' i.e. a parish of origin. 'In this parish' or 'in' a place most usually refers to a tenancy or short term presence in an area.

(i) Births and baptisms

The established church OPRs tended for the most part to record baptisms rather than births, as these were more important to the minister, though some recorded both. A good record will list the child's name along with that of his father and mother (including her maiden name), the father's occupation and place of abode, and if lucky, the names of witnesses to the baptism. At worst, you may simply find the name of the father and the fact that he had a son or a daughter, with the baptismal date recorded but with no Christian name for the child ('had a son' or 'had a daughter'), and no details for the mother.

If a child was illegitimate, this can be recorded in many ways, with the child potentially being described as 'natural born', 'bastard child', or just plain 'illegitimate'. If you find such an entry, make sure to check the kirk session records in the NAS. You will likely find an investigation into who the father was, and in some cases, you might even get an answer.

It may be that when looking for a birth or baptism you will not find it, for which there could be many reasons. The first is that it may have simply not been recorded. From 1783 to 1794, the Stamp Act required that all births in Britain should be taxed at a rate of three pence when recorded in the registers, with a similar charge for all marriage and burial records. As a result, many people refused to register. It is also true that by the 19th century, many people were giving up on the Church, with some established kirk parishes perhaps recording as few as a third of the events actually happening in their area, though this was partly because so many people had deserted them for the dissenting or nonconformist churches. With the arrival of civil registration in 1855, many people wished to retrospectively record an earlier baptism, and as such, this entry may have been listed in the *Register of Neglected Entries*, if the birth could be proved from other sources to have happened between 1801 and 1854. These are integrated into the OPR births sections of the respective ScotlandsPeople databases.

Some people did get baptised, but not necessarily just after birth. You may find examples where several children from the same family were all baptised at the same time. Although tempted to think that they might have been twins or triplets etc, the census records, or later death records, may tell another story. You may also find an entry hastily scribbled into a margin or at the foot of a page – it may be that it was simply omitted and hastily inserted, or may have been placed there many years later. If so, it may again be evidence of a simple omission, or possibly suggest that the event was initially registered within a different church denomination and subsequently recorded into the established church register following a change in the religious adherence of the particular individuals concerned.

Often you will find some fascinating local trends in records. In the parish of Glass in Aberdeenshire, the witnesses attending baptisms shared the Christian names of the children being christened, as in the following examples:

> *May 29th 1773 Thomas Brander in Cairnmore wt his wife Christian Strachan had a son baptized called George before these witnesses George Brander in Cairnmore & George Taylor in Cairnborrow.*

(Source: Glass OPR B 199/00 29 MAR 1773)

> *March 29th 1787 Thos Brander in Cairnmore with his wife Christian Strachan had a son baptized called Alexander before these witnesses Alexander Simpson and Alexr. Louper both in Cairnmore.*

(Source: Glass OPR B 199/00 Fr. 85 29 MAR 1787)

The context within which entries are recorded in an OPR register can often therefore be as interesting as the information in the entry itself.

Naming patterns

A traditional naming pattern was in operation in Scotland, which worked as follows:

The eldest son named after the father's father
The second son named after the mother's father
The third son named after the father
The eldest daughter named after the mother's mother
The second daughter named after the father's mother
The third daughter named after the mother.

This was not a hard and fast rule, but can often be used to help predict the names of a child's grandparents. There were some regional variations – in 18th century Bute, for example, the eldest daughter was often named after the paternal grandmother and the second daughter after the maternal grandmother. Complications occasionally cropped up also in situations such as both parents having mothers or fathers with the same names. If you find two or more children with the same name born to a couple, this usually means that the first died in infancy. You might also find that a child is named after a newly arrived minister to a parish, or some other influential individual.

(ii) Marriages and banns

There were many ways in Scotland that a couple could marry, but the only truly legal way was to do so through the established Church. There were other ways however which although not legal, were deemed valid and therefore tolerated. People could marry by declaration, with or without witnesses, and without any involvement of a minister at all ('declaration de presenti'), or they could live together as if they were married, without ever actually marking the commitment through a ceremony. A tourist pamphlet in the 19th century, entitled *Matrimonial Guide Through Scotland*, summed it up neatly:

> Suppose that young Jocky or Jenny,
> Say "We two are husband and wife."
> The witnesses needn't be many,
> They're instantly buckled for life.

These were known as 'irregular' marriages, and whenever discovered, the Church would haul up the guilty parties in front of the kirk session, then fine and rebuke them. A useful article by Bruce Durie on Scottish marriages in their various forms has been published in the eleventh edition of the *Family and Local History Handbook*, entitled 'Regular and Irregular Marriages' (2008, **www.genealogical.co.uk**).

Normally a record within a kirk register will show the calling of the banns, which were required to be announced three times prior to a wedding, in order to allow any objections to be heard. An example is as follows, from the parish of Tarves in Aberdeenshire, in 1747:

Novr 1st Findlay & Barron

The Matrimonial Banns of Patrick ffindlay in this parish & Margaret Barron in the parish of Meldry were proclaimed p 1mo

(Source: OPR M 243/00 1 Nov 1747 Tarves)

You may find separate banns entries within two separate parishes, for each of the contracting parties. Many entries just list the first time the banns were called, but some will also follow through with the date that the marriage actually happened, and even list witnesses. Sometimes the banns were called three times on the same day. It was also traditional to marry within the parish of the bride, either at the church, a manse, a local hotel or inn, or even the family home.

Occasionally the only evidence that you might find of a marriage that was about to take place is the record of 'pledge money' or 'contract money' in the kirk session records. This was basically a deposit given to the session prior to a marriage to guarantee that it would take place, which would be returned after the event with a suitable deduction made for the poor of the parish. The following is the record of such a payment made by my five times great grandparents at Perth:

Perth the twenty third day of April 1772
Contract money
From John Paton and Ann Watson Three shillings and fourpence

(Source: NAS CH2/521/21/439)

In this case I was fortunate to find both a record for the marriage in the register and the pledge money in the session minutes. A word of caution though – whilst the payment may have been made or the banns called, this does not necessarily mean that the wedding actually happened!

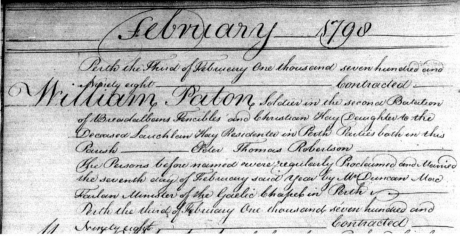

The wedding record of four times great grandparents William Paton and Christian Hay.

In England and Wales, Hardwicke's Act of 1753 banned irregular marriages in dissenting churches south of the border, requiring all weddings to be carried out by a minister of the established faith. This never applied to Scotland, and hence why so many couples from down south flocked over the border to places such as Gretna to have an irregular marriage performed. Registers of the marriages at the Queens Head Inn at Gretna from June 1843 to February 1862 can be consulted on microfilm at the ScotlandsPeople Center (MR 103/1-5), at the NAS, or in bound photocopied volumes at Gretna Registration Office, Central Avenue, Gretna (tel: 01461 337648), and at the Ewart Library on Catherine Street, Dumfries (tel: 01387 253820). An index to 4500 Gretna marriages from 1795 to 1895 has been placed online by Achievements Ltd at **www.achievements.co.uk/ services/gretna/index.php** - a search returns only the names of the bride and groom, with a full look up based on the result then costing £15. The indexes are also available at **www.ancestry.co.uk**.

Tip: The 'dead' language...

Latin phrases you may commonly encounter within records of marriage banns include 'pro primo' (pro 1mo), 'pro secundo' (pro 2do) or 'pro tertio' (pro 3io), meaning 'for the first time', 'for the second time' and 'for the third time', as well as 'eodem die', meaning 'on the same day'. You will also find phrases such as 'on the 13th instant', meaning in the current month, or 'on the 15th ultimo', meaning the previous month.

An Irregular Scottish Marriage

The following is an interesting piece from the Caledonian Mercury of March 5th 1838 which highlights the intricacies of the law surrounding a Scottish marriage!

MARRIAGE FRAUD – A rather singular case was brought before Mr. Sheriff Barclay on Wednesday by the Procurator Fiscal, against Peter Thomson, farmer, Tilliepourie. The pannel was convicted of fraud and wilful imprisonment, having deceived the Rev. Thomas Buchanan, Logierait, and induced him to marry the pannel to a woman, with whom there had been no proclamation of banns. Proclamation of banns between Thompson and Mary Scott at Grandtully had been made, but on calling at Mr. Buchanan's manse with the certificates of that proclamation to have the ceremony of marriage performed, the bride, instead of being Mary Scott, was another woman of the name of Catherine Robertson, who resides at Derculich, and whom he represented to be the lady, Mary Scott, whose name was on the certificate. The Sheriff fined the pannel five pounds. Notwithstanding the deception practised on the clergyman, the marriage, it is considered, is valid by the law of Scotland.

(iii) *Deaths and Burials*

There was no requirement on the part of Scottish ministers to keep death or burial registers, though many did. Some of the records provide direct evidence of death, in the form of the actual date that an individual passed away. Others may provide more indirect proof in the form of the burial date, or of a payment for the use of a mortcloth, which was a shroud hired from the church to cover the coffin prior to burial. It is sometimes impossible to note from the record exactly what the date refers to, and the listed details can be extremely limited, though some parishes did provide considerably more information, such as a cause of death and occupation.

The deaths that have survived in the OPRs can be accessed on microfilm at a local library, LDS family history centre or archive, and have also been digitised and made accessible at the ScotlandsPeople website. They will be made available for consultation at the ScotlandsPeople Centre, though can be consulted on microfilm there in the meantime.

Always be extremely cautious when using these records, as they are very patchy and can in most cases be very hard to confirm as the entry you require, unless you can find corroborating evidence elsewhere, such as in a will, obituary or monumental inscription.

Additional burial records

In many cases the only record of death you might find will be a monumental inscription, essentially a carving on a gravestone which has recorded the date of death and other useful genealogical information. One of the greatest contributions made by Scotland's community of family history societies over the years has been the many transcription projects that they have carried out across the country, recording these epitaphs for posterity. Often such transcriptions may be the only record surviving, with the stones having since fallen or eroded and no longer legible. If a graveyard has been recorded twice in two different time periods it is worth consulting both records, as information which may be missing in one might turn up in another.

Most family history societies sell CDs and/or booklets with such inscriptions, and they can also be found as collections in various repositories such as the ScotlandsPeople Centre, the Scottish Genealogy Society or at the Mitchell Library in Glasgow. A useful guide for working out which graveyards have been recorded is the Scottish Association of Family History Societies' CD *Inventory of Scottish Graveyards* (2nd edition, 2008).

There are other volunteer groups recording graveyards. These include the Recording Angels project (**www.recordingangels.org.uk**), which is working

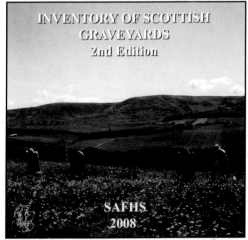

The extremely useful Inventory of Scottish Graveyards CD from SAFHS

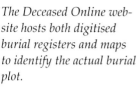

*The Deceased Online web-
site hosts both digitised
burial registers and maps
to identify the actual burial
plot.*

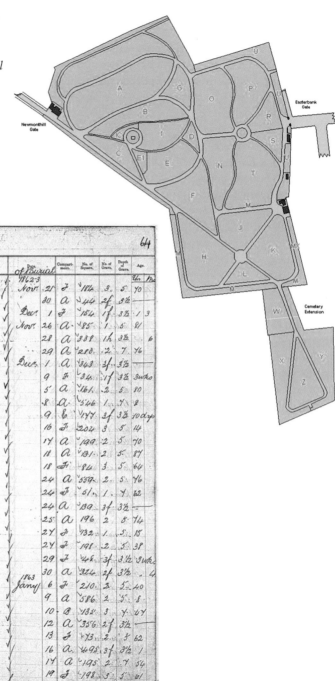

No.	NAME.	Date of Burial.	Compartment.	No. of Square.	No. of Grave.	Depth of Grave.	Age.
		1862-3					Yrs Mo
2014	Eliz. Ormond or Grieve	Nov. 21	F	184	3	5	70
5	Alex. Murdoch's child	30	a	44	2f	3½	
6	Wm. Anderson	Dec. 1	F	154	1f	3½	1 3
7	Susan Duncan	Nov. 26	a	85	1	5	81
8	James Samson	28	a	338	1h	3½	6
9	Mary McNicoll	29	a	288	2	7	76
2020	Alex. Limes child	Dec. 1	a	343	3f	3½	
1	James Nicoll's child	9	F	34	1f	3½	3wks
2	Wm. Reid	5	a	161	2	5	80
3	Robert Walker	8	a	546	1	7	8
4	Archd. Stupart	9	E	477	3f	3½	10 dys
5	James Kydd	16	F	204	3	5	14
6	Carnegie Addison	17	a	199	2	5	70
7	John Stirling	18	a	131	2	5	87
8	George Barry	18	F	84	3	5	64
9	Alex. Gibson	24	a	559	2	5	76
2030	Helen Hutton	24	F	51	1	4	62
1	James Campbell's child	24	a	139	3f	3½	—
2	Mary Fairweather	25	a	196	2	8	74
3	George Kinnear	27	F	132	1	5	15
4	Barbara Farquharson	27	F	198	2	5	38
5	Charles Bruce	29	F	48	3f	3½	3wks
6	Jessie H. Donald	30	a	224	2f	3½	4
7	Charles Porter	1863 Jany 6	F	210	3	5	40
8	David Watt	9	a	586	2	5	8
9	John Smith	10	B	132	3	7	47
2040	James Moffat's child	12	a	356	2f	3½	
1	Wm. Ross	13	F	73	2	5	62
2	Joseph Carruthers	16	a	495	3f	3½	1
3	Jean Holmes or Benoon	17	a	195	2	7	54
4	Alex. Guild	19	F	198	3	5	61
5	Agnes Japp	20	a	207	2	5	30

on the preservation of information found within cemeteries in the Midlothian area, and the Moray Burial Research Group (**www.mbgrg.org**), covering the area of Morayshire. Some local family history websites provide an online index to their monumental inscriptions on their websites, which can be useful (see Appendix 2), whilst the *Memento Mori* website at **www.memento-mori.co.uk** has indices to many graveyards mainly in the Central Belt, which can be used to order up photographs of individual gravestones at a reasonable price.

Additional web based resources for burials include an index to Edinburgh's Greyfriars cemetery from 1715 to 1825 at the World Burial Index (**www.worldburial index.com**), and a database of 14,000 burials extracted from the OPRs by Shauna C. Anderson at Brigham Young University, available at World Vital Records (**www.world vitalrecords.com**), covering the following parishes - Cockpen, Midlothian; Cranston; Crichton; Dalkeith; Dunfermline, Fife; Edinburgh; Fala; Gladsmuir; Heriot; Humbie; Newbattle; Pencaitland, Midlothian; Prestonpans, East Lothian; Salton; Shotts; Tranent and East Lothian.

It is also worth bearing in mind that many county records offices have additional burial registers for local municipal cemeteries, particularly, but not exclusively, for the post 1855 period. Some of these can be found online, for example burial registers for Perth from 1794 can be found at the Perth and Kinross Archives website, whilst Dundee's Howff Cemetery records can be found at the Friends of Dundee Archives site at **www.fdca.org.uk**.

More recently, the pay per view Deceased Online website at **www.deceased online.com** has started releasing Scottish records, with the first to be uploaded sourced from Angus. The site provides access to digitised entries from burial registers, information on others buried within the same lair, and in many cases provides location maps showing where the burial took place. In due course it is also planned that photographs of some stones will be placed online. The records uploaded so far include:

Arbroath Eastern Cemetery	25 DEC 1894 – 16 OCT 2003
Arbroath Western Cemetery	31 OCT 1867 – 27 DEC 2003
Brechin Cemetery	26 OCT 1857 – 18 DEC 2007
Kirriemuir Cemetery	30 MAR 1858 – 17 JAN 2008
Newmonthill Cemetery	14 MAY 1850 – 30 AUG 1985
Sleepyhillock Cemetery	5 JAN 1895 – 7 JAN 2008

At the time of writing, a further 80,000 records for Angus, including for Brechin Cathedral, were also imminently due for publication on the site.

The History of the Kirk

The Church of Scotland was established following the Scottish Reformation instituted by the firebrand preacher John Knox in 1560. For its first century of existence, up to 1688, it had a long and bloody history, as various forces in the country, from kings to Covenanters, tried to impose their style of worship upon it.

The problem lay in the completely incompatible styles of worship being promoted, namely Episcopacy and Presbyterianism. The Church of England is Episcopal – it has a hierarchy, where local ministers are overseen by bishops, then archbishops and finally the monarch as the head. Swap the monarch for the Pope, and you have a similar structural set up for the Roman Catholic Church. In Presbyterianism, the minister was answerable to his congregation only, and there were no bishops, making it difficult for the monarch to assert any form of control. With the Union of the Crowns in 1603, this did not go down too well, and the Stuarts kings tried to enforce episcopacy within Scotland at various points in the 17th century, ultimately leading to the English Civil War, the struggles of the Covenanters and latterly the Killing Times towards the end of the century (Ancestry hosts the Scottish Covenanters Index of over 26,000 names, as compiled by Isabelle McLean Drown, at www.ancestry.co.uk). The Presbyterian form of worship was finally established at the 'Glorious Revolution' of 1688.

Presbyterians loved a good doctrinal argument though, particularly over the point of patronage, the right to decide who could appoint a minister to a congregation. Landowners believed it was their right; many congregations disagreed. Over time, some ministers began to perceive a drift away from the original Calvinist concept of a 'Godly Commonwealth', where the Church was in de facto control of the State, though others were happy to bow to their patrons. This led to various secession churches being created in the 18th Century, as various congregations simply left the establishment. By the 19th Century two wings had formed within the main Church of Scotland, the Evangelists and the Moderates, with the former faction attempting to turn the clock back. Matters came to a head in 1843 with the Disruption, when the Evangelists walked out to form the Free Church of Scotland. Their timing could not have been worse from their own theological point of view, as it happened right in the middle of the Irish Famine, when thousands of Irishmen were flocking into Scotland, and dramatically re-establishing Roman Catholicism in the country. The Disruption ultimately weakened both wings of the Church, and despite an eventual reunification in 1929, it allowed a secular State to ultimately emerge triumphant.

Kirk Sessions Records

Whilst the state is today responsible for the education of our children, welfare payments and law and order, much of this was previously the role of the Church of Scotland. Within each parish, a kirk session would oversee matters such as discipline, Sunday school education, poor relief, and the election of the minister. The session members were elected annually from the congregation, and in theory provided a democratic basis for the running of the kirk.

The records of kirk sessions can be a fascinating source for stories and material concerning your ancestor, as well as information on the parish's day to day affairs. If, for example, you have a child known to have been illegitimate in your tree, there is a very strong chance that his or her parents were hauled up before the session to be rebuked and fined. Depending on the minister, elder or clerk concerned, there could be pages and pages of investigation into the alleged paternity of the child, or a simple notice merely indicating that somebody had appeared before the session on a charge of 'antenuptial fornication'. The following example from Arbroath in October 1791 concerns a man called Thomas Dogood (Ducat or Duckett), who had previously been up before the session on a similar charge just two years earlier:

> *The Session being met and constituted sederunt Minister and Elders. There appeared before this meeting Thomas Dogood & acknowledged that he is the father of Elizabeth Blair's Child which she brought forth in the Month of Septr 1790 he was sharply rebuked for his Sin & Scandal, this being a relapse, & ordered to pay a Fine of fifteen Shillings for the Use of the poor, and appointed to appear publickly tomorrow to be rebuked before the Congregation and in Consideration that he is now married & lives at a considerable distance, the Session agreed that he be absolved & dismissed tomorrow, he paid his fine immediately.*

(Source: NAS CH2/1414/2/263)

The session minutes are also useful for identifying some financial transactions, such as contract or pledge money for marriages or mortcloth payments. Sometimes parishioners could obtain a bond from the session and pay it back within an agreed time frame. Until 1845 the kirk was also responsible for the care of the poor, and made regular payments to them from the money raised in its weekly subscriptions. The information given in the records again varies from parish to parish, and in many cases the names of the poor are not included, just the amounts paid out. Occasionally you may also be fortunate to find a note of a 'testificate', a testimonial brought by an incomer to a parish, or given to a parishioner when leaving the parish, which can help to identify the movement of your ancestors from one parish to another.

Beyond the strictly genealogical assistance that these records can offer, kirk session minutes can also help to illustrate how a parish operated, providing many other interesting items of news. The following are two entries from the Aberdeenshire parish of Fyvie in 1787:

> *29 July 1787*
>
> *After Sermon the Monthly Distrn was made. As there is now at the Manse a considerable quantity of bad & counterfeit half-pence that have for some time past been picked out of the weekly Collections, the Session requested that the Minr would send them to Aberdeen & cause them to be melted down in order to prevent their circulation*

30 Sep 1787

The Minr acquainted the Session that he had sent the bad copper to Aberdeen but had not yet been informed of the value. The Session considering that there were only five Communion cups in this parish, & that for some time past it has been necessary to borrow other five from a neighbouring Parish, requested the Minr to cause five metal cups to be made in Aberdeen for that purpose.

(Source: NAS CH2/1152/1/33 Fyvie)

Having received a dodgy consignment of counterfeit coins over several weeks, the elders basically instructed the minister to 'waste not, want not'!

Not all kirk session minutes have survived down the years, with some having been damaged or lost, and others deliberately destroyed. The vast majority of surviving kirk session books are held at the NAS, where they have been digitised and made available to view in the Historical Search Room at HM General Register House and in the West Search Room at West Register House. The NAS catalogue can be consulted to see which records are held. A major project by the Scottish Documents project (**www.scottish documents.com**) is currently under way at the time of writing to digitise further materials from the 20,000 or so volumes of church court records, including further materials from the records of the presbyteries, synods and annual General Assembly of the Church of Scotland, as well as the secession churches. Initially this will be a service provided through the search rooms of a dozen or so archives across Scotland which hold church court records and which are working in partnership with the project. If the trial is successful a full service is intended for launch in 2010, which promises to revolutionise the way that we currently access such materials.

Some further sets of kirk session minutes are also held by the GROS, contained within the church registers for births and marriages which it holds. They can be examined on microfilm at the ScotlandsPeople Centre, with a full listing of the records available at **www.scotlandspeoplehub.gov.uk/pdf/list-of-oprs-appendix2.pdf**. Other records survive in archives around the country, and can be sourced through the Scottish Archive Network at **www.scan.org.uk**.

Increasingly, records are also being transcribed and/or indexed, and made available through family history society publications, as well as on the internet. A good example is a website from the Friends of the Archives of Dumfries and Galloway at **www.dg community.net/historicalindexes**, which contains indexes to the kirk session minutes from Dumfries (1689-1838), Troqueer (1698-1771) and Mouswald (1640-1659).

Tip: Handwriting

Whilst the kirk session records at the NAS have been digitised to an exceptionally high standard, they may still be difficult to decipher, simply because of the handwriting. For earlier records, particularly for the 16th and 17th centuries, the styles of handwriting used can often be unrecognisable to the modern eye. A useful website to help you read the unreadable is www.scottishhandwriting.com, which offers free online tutorials. If a single word is illegible, it is also worth looking at other words on the page written in the same handwriting style to try to compare individual letters one at time.

Other Protestant Denominations

There were, and still are, many other religious denominations in Scotland, including dissenting Presbyterian sects, Methodists, Baptists and the Scottish Episcopal Church. You may actually find that the events of some of these other churches are recorded in the established church OPRs. As the 'official' church, its ministers often felt it was their responsibility to record all births or baptisms in their vicinity. In most cases, if you cannot find the record in an established church register, you will need to look for the register of the dissenting congregation. Most of these have been deposited at the NAS and can be searched for using the online catalogue, though some do remain in regional archives across the country.

Records for particular denominations can be found under the following NAS accession numbers, with the year noted for the foundation of each:

Associate Synod	1733	CH3
Relief Church	1761	CH3
General Associate Synod (Antiburgher)	1747	CH3
Associate Synod (Burgher)	1747	CH3
United Association Secession	1820	CH3
Original Secession Synod	1827	CH3
Free Church of Scotland	1843	CH3 & CH13
United Free Church	(post 1929)	CH13

A useful book summarising the locations of surviving records of births and marriages from these denominations is Diane Baptie's *Registers of the Secession Churches of Scotland*, published by the Scottish Association of Family History Societies in August 2000. This lists holdings in other archives across the country in addition to those found at the NAS. For a chart showing the formation of the various branches of the church, visit **http://website.lineone.net/~davghalgh/churchhistory.html**.

Records for some other religious denominations are held under the following source numbers at NAS, though do check the SCAN catalogue (Chapter 2) for any local holdings located elsewhere in the country:

Quakers (Society of Friends)	CH10/1-4
Methodists	CH11
Scottish Episcopal Church	CH12
Catholic Apostolic Church (Irvingites)	RH4/174

In order to identify which dissenting denominations existed in a parish, you should start by consulting the Statistical Accounts of Scotland and other gazetteers for the area (see Chapter 8).

Roman Catholicism

Records of the Roman Catholic Church can be sourced from the Scottish Catholic Archives in Edinburgh at **www.scottishcatholicarchives.org.uk**. Copies of all their baptismal and marriage registers are held by the NAS (CH21), and are being made available at the ScotlandsPeople Centre and website throughout 2010, along with various other records such as deaths and burials, confirmations, lists of communicants, sick calls, lists of converts, first confessions, sent rents and 'status animarum' records ('state of the soul', a form of church census), and records from the Bishopric of the Forces from Britain and overseas. A list of the surviving registers, and their years of coverage, can be consulted in the Family History section of the SCA website, which also hosts a family history discussion forum, which may be of assistance. Baptismal records from Braemar (1703-1757) and Braemar and Glengair (1781 -1845) are available in the UK Parish Records Collection at Ancestry.co.uk.

Despite the Reformation of 1560, Roman Catholicism survived in many Highland based parishes, but the majority of the records refer to parishes in existence from the 1840s onwards, after the flood of migrants from Ireland's famine stricken land dramatically re-invigorated the Church's congregations. It is in fact well worth consulting Catholic baptismal records after the advent of civil registration in 1855, as they usually list godparents, often siblings of the baby's parents, which may provide extra clues when trying to establish from where in Ireland your ancestor might have originated. Other more notable waves of more recent immigration have included Italians, including the Nardini family of Largs in North Ayrshire, and Lithuanian and Polish Catholics, many of whom were based in Lanarkshire and worshipped at the Carfin Grotto near Motherwell (**www.carfin.org.uk**).

Judaism

The first Jewish synagogue opened in Scotland was that at Garnethill, Glasgow, in 1879. The building is located at 127 Hill Street, Glasgow G3 6UB, and today hosts the Scottish Jewish Archive Centre (**www.sjac.org.uk**), which was established in 1987. Amongst its holdings is the *Historical Database of Scottish Jewry*, which contains information from the 18th Century up to the 1920s derived from many sources, such as synagogue, cemetery and naturalisation records, documenting well over 16,000 individuals. The centre can be visited by appointment only each Friday between 9.30am and 1.00pm, or without appointment on the monthly open day, held on a Sunday between 2.00pm and 4.00pm – check the centre for details by calling (0141) 332 4911.

The Scottish Jewish Archive Centre in Glasgow.

Further information on Jewish sources in Scotland can be consulted at the Jewish Genealogical Society of Great Britain's website at **www.jgsgb.org.uk/scot01.shtml**, whilst other useful websites include the JewishGen site at **www.jewishgen.org** and the Yad Vashem site at **www.yadvashem.org**, which includes a database of over three million Shoah victims' names from the Jewish Holocaust of World War Two.

Islam

For those with Islamic roots in Scotland, there is no formal history centre or society within the country dealing with the history of the Muslim population. The majority of Muslims are recent immigrants to the country, having mainly arrived after the Second World War, though some have roots much further back. The first Muslim student in the country, for example, was Wazir Beg, who studied medicine at the University of Edinburgh in the 1850s. The majority of early Muslims were maritime workers known as 'lascars', working in the import trade in cities such as Glasgow and Dundee, and particularly prevalent within industries such as jute manufacturing.

Whilst there is no dedicated organisation, a useful first port of call is the Scottish Islamic Foundation at 5 Royal Exchange Square, Glasgow, G1 3AH. It can also be contacted at (0141) 890112, or its website consulted at **www.scottishislamic.org**.

Sikhs

Sikhs are another relatively recent group to have settled in Scotland, with most having arrived in the late 20th century. The first Gurdwara (the Sikh place of worship) was set up in Glasgow's South Portland Street in the 1920s, and today there are Sikh communities in Glasgow, Edinburgh and Dundee. However, individual Sikhs have lived in Scotland from the mid 19th century, including Maharajah Duleep Singh, also known as the 'Black Prince of Perthshire', who settled in the county in 1854, and who took up residence temporarily at Castle Menzies where he was famed for his extravagant lifestyle.

For those with Sikh ancestors in Scotland, two useful sites are the Scottish history section of the Sikhs in Scotland website at **www.asht.info/trail/r/1/scotland**, and the Scottish section of the Anglo-Sikh Heritage Trail site at **www.asht.info/trail/r/1/scotland**.

Further Reading

ANON (2003) *The Sword and the Cross: Four Turbulent Episodes in the History of Christian Scotland*. Edinburgh: St. Andrew Press.

BAPTIE, Dianne (2000) *Registers of the Secession Churches in Scotland: records of Baptisms, Marriages and Deaths in the Scottish Secession Churches (including Lists of Members)*. Edinburgh: Scottish Association of Family History Societies.

BROWN, Calum G (1997) *Religion and Society in Scotland since 1707*. Edinburgh: Edinburgh University Press

KURZWEIL, Arthur (2004) *From Generation to Generation: How to Trace Your Jewish Genealogy and Family History*. San Francisco: Jossey-Bass.

LOVE, Dane (2000), *Scottish Covenanter Stories: Tales from the Killing Times*. Glasgow: Neil Wilson Publishing.

5. *The Church of Jesus Christ of Latter Day Saints*

The Church of Jesus Christ of Latter-Day Saints, known more commonly as the Mormon Church, is a worldwide Christian religion with over 13 million members. Founded in 1830 by Joseph Smith Junior, its followers have for decades been at the forefront of efforts to create new genealogical resources for research.

Mormons believe that the dead must be baptised retrospectively in what are known as 'vicarious', 'proxy' or 'temple' baptisms, which they deem an essential ordinance for those who may not have had the chance for a baptism before their death, with the belief being that only the baptised can enter the Kingdom of God. Performed by full immersion in a temple font, a living person is baptised as a proxy for a deceased ancestor, though men can only act for deceased males and women for deceased females. There is a common belief outside the Mormon faith that the church 'makes' ancestors convert to their religion through such baptisms, but in fact the church believes that ancestors are free to accept or reject these vicarious baptisms in the afterlife.

The church also preaches that family relationships can be preserved beyond death, through its 'sealing' ordinance. Whilst a civil marriage in the church's eyes may end at death, those whose unions have been 'sealed' will remain bound for all eternity. However, sealings are not only solely linked to marriages, they are used to eternally bind the relationships of parents to children, adoptive children, and other family based relationships.

It is because of these two religious doctrines that so much effort has been put into creating the world's largest resource of family history materials. Helpfully for genealogists, much of this material is being made available through initiatives such as the International Genealogical Index, the FamilySearch website (**www.familysearch.org**), and a growing worldwide network of family history centres. All operate under the auspices of the Genealogical Society of Utah, founded in 1894.

The International Genealogical Index (IGI)

In 1969 the Mormons created a massive database known as the *International Genealogical Index*, or IGI, to replace its *Temple Records Index Bureau*, which acted as a guide for identifying baptisms and other ordinances that had been performed within the church. The IGI includes an index to Church of Scotland OPR records for baptisms and marriages up to 1854, as well as for some dissenting church records, though none will be found for Scottish Roman Catholic Church events, with the church having a serious theological objection to the Mormon project. The index also covers records of statutory birth and marriage registration from 1855 up to 1875.

The IGI is available at the ScotlandsPeople Centre in both CD-ROM format and through the FamilySearch website on the centre's many terminals, with the database located at **www.familysearch.org/eng/Search/frameset_search.asp**. Both versions of the index can also be found at various libraries and societies across the country, and the online version can of course be consulted from home. The major difference between the different formats is that the CDs stopped being updated in the 1990s, whereas the online version continues to be expanded

The *International Genealogical Index* is just that – an index. Never take the details for granted from the site without consulting the original record. In some cases you might be surprised at what is not recorded. The following information is found in the IGI entry for the baptism of a person called Margaretta BROWN in Perth:

Margaretta Sarah Tyrwhill Brown, female

Christening:	*26 DEC 1807 Perth, Perth, Scotland*
Father	*Jonathan Brown*
Mother	*Julia Anna Craddock*

Batch No: C119476 Dates: 1806-1812 Source Call No: 1040159 Type: Film
Printout Call No: 6902908 Type: Film

Now have a look at what the original OPR entry actually states:

Perth the Twenty first day of October One thousand and eight hundred and seven years was born

Margaretta Sarah Tyrwhill Brown Eldest lawful Daughter to Jonathan Brown from New Brunswick British America Captain of the Seventy Fifth Regiment of Foot, and Julia Anna Cradock his spouse, Daughter to Marmaduke Cradock of the Parish of Gainsford County of Durham, Margaret Waddington his spouse, daughter to Sheldon Cradock Nowforth Deceased, and, Sarah Williamson his spouse, great Granddaughter by the Mothers side to Sir John Tyrwhill deceased of Haysfield county of Lincoln. The above named Margaretta was baptized the twenty sixth December said year by the Reverend Dr Grant Minister of the Episcopal Congregation at Dundee.

(Source: OPR 387/14 p.144)

What started as a single record in the IGI identifying two generations in fact turns out to have information on eight generations within the family! Normally the original information is not as detailed as this example, which is somewhat exceptional, but you may find useful clues about residence or occupation within an original OPR record which will not be included in the IGI entry.

As shown above, records are indexed with a batch number which can be viewed at the bottom of the entry. These batch numbers are in fact a useful way to search for all those sharing the surname that you are interested in within a parish, if you are carrying out a one-name study or looking for other instances of a name within your family's immediate location at any given time. By typing in the surname, and then the batch number and region (British Isles), all index entries bearing that name will be returned for that microfilm. To obtain the batch numbers for a parish's baptism or marriage registers, visit Hugh Wallis' excellent website at **http://freepages.genealogy.rootsweb.ancestry.com/ ~hughwallis/IGIBatchNumbers.htm**.

The IGI entries for Scotland can also be examined through the Scots Origins website, with the added bonus that searches can be done at the parish level, which is not possible on the FamilySearch site without the batch numbers. For births and christenings, use **www.originsnetwork.com/scotsorigins/SOSearchBC.aspx**, and for marriages, visit **www.originsnetwork.com/scotsorigins/SOSearchMar.aspx**.

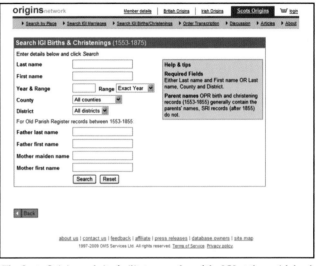

There is another useful trick with the IGI, which allows you to find the children of a particular couple. Type the names of the two parents in the search fields on the right hand side of the screen, and narrow down the location, then click 'Search'. The returned results will be for all children recorded in the IGI to that couple (or couples if the names are common). You do not need to put the mother's surname in if it is not known – many parish records only

The Scots Origins website facilitates searches of the IGI at the parish level.

list the mother by first name, and some not at all. Conversely, you can also do a search for a child with a mother's name only, if you do not know the father's name, or if you suspect that a child may have been illegitimate.

It is worth pointing out that I have in the past found additional children to a couple within the OPR records that the IGI did not list, and you may also find that there was more than one couple sharing the names of the parents that you are searching for.

When used correctly, the IGI can be an incredibly useful shortcut. A word of caution on the wider FamilySearch database however – the site does not check patron submissions when they publish them. So as with any other secondary source, if you find a tree online that takes somebody back to Robert the Bruce or the Lord God Almighty himself, make sure you have corroborated the original entries before leaping for joy and taking the records at face value and integrating them into your tree.

Other FamilySearch databases

There are other databases that can be searched through the FamilySearch site, including Ancestral File and Pedigree Resource File. These are indexed entries derived from submitted trees by the church's members, and without consulting the original microfilms, which contain copies of the original research, it is impossible to gauge whether they are accurate. As such, the original records for these entries should also be consulted. The Record Search pilot website at **http://pilot.familysearch.org** is a further site worth keeping an eye on over the next few years. The Mormons are currently digitising and indexing vast swathes of records held at the Granite Mountain vault in Utah, and the results are being placed on this site free of charge to access. There are already many American and Canadian censuses on the site, as well as some English and Irish records (including indexes to statutory Irish births, marriages and deaths), and it will be only a matter of time before Scottish material also finds its way there. The significant advantage here is that many of the records being digitised are the original documents, or at least taken from microfilmed photographs of the original documents.

Family History centres

There are currently sixteen family history centres run by the LDS Church in Scotland, located in Aberdeen, Alloa, Ayr, Dumfries, Dundee, Edinburgh, Elgin, Glasgow, Invergordon, Inverness, Kirkcaldy, Lerwick, Montrose, Motherwell, Paisley and Stornoway. Within these centres it is possible to view the Church's collections, though you may have to order them up in advance for a fee. Details of your nearest centre can be found at **www.familysearch.org/eng/library/FHC/frameset_fhc.asp**. Through these centres you can order up and view microfilms of many Scottish records, not just of the vital records,

The LDS Family History Centre in Glasgow.

but maps, sasines, valuation rolls and more. Each centre also has particular regional strengths, such as additional local history books held for that area.

The source information needed to order up the correct records exists not only within the IGI and the Church's other databases, but also through its online catalogue at **www.familysearch.org/eng/Library/FHLC/frameset_fhlc.asp**. This details many thousands of valuable record collections, some of which are not indexed, and is searchable by placename, family names, authors and subjects. For example, if I do a keyword search on 'Inverness', after I have confirmed that it is Inverness in Scotland that I am interested in, I then come across a long list of records for the parish, city and county. If I then click on 'Inverness - Probate Records', I find that I can order up a range of books and microfilms listing probate records for the county from 1630 to 1877. Another very useful addition to the FamilySearch portfolio is its Wiki site at **https://wiki.family-search.org/en/Scotland**, which provides a virtual online encyclopaedia of its Scottish holdings, with some very useful background information.

As with many institutions, the staff will not do your research for you, but will be only too happy to show you how to use their facilities and how to order microfilms and microfiche.

6. Censuses and Substitutes

A census has been carried out in Scotland every ten years from 1801, with the exception of 1941, when the Second World War provided a more pressing national priority. The censuses for 1801 to 1831 were largely statistical affairs, though a few parish ministers did in fact enumerate their local populations by name, with some of these lists surviving. The first genuinely useful census, however, is that for 1841, and at present, Scottish returns from 1841 to 1901 are available to view online.

The censuses are important documents as they allow us to drop in on our ancestors every ten years to see how they are getting on. They can help us to find out what they did for a living, where they were born, who they were married to, how many children they had, various addresses at which they might have lived, career moves, and so much more. It is important to remember, however, that we are literally dropping in on them for just one night. Whilst a couple may be noted in two subsequent censuses as having five children, that is not to say that they did not have more in between – they may have had a child who died in infancy, for example, or another who may have been off working as a servant somewhere and therefore not at home on census night.

From 1801 to 1851 the census was co-ordinated by the Home Office in London, but from 1861, the Registrar General for Scotland became responsible for the returns north of the border. The registration districts in Scotland were initially based on parish boundaries, making it easier to marry up the vital records and the equivalent census entries for the area.

Always be in awe of a census entry – this is after all a snapshot of your family from a bygone era that you are looking at – but don't always trust it! Ages can be exaggerated, birthplace names may change between different returns, recording and transcription errors may creep in, and your ancestors may have even lied about some of the information given – assuming they bothered to fill out a schedule form in the first place. But taken in conjunction with the OPR and civil registration records, the census is the third side of the basic triangle to help you build your initial family tree.

The following is a breakdown of what to expect in each of the censuses.

1841 Census

Recorded on the night of June 6th, the 1841 census is a bit of an oddity, in that it is something of a half way measure between the purely statistical censuses that preceded it, and the considerably more detailed records which followed in subsequent decades. It contains the following useful information:

- Boundary information, in the form of the parish name, noted at the top of the page

- Place of residence, usually a village, farm or street
- Whether the house was inhabited or uninhabited
- Age – with males in the left age column, females in the right. In most areas this is rounded down to the nearest multiple of 5 for adults over the age of 15. In other words, a 29 year old could very well be listed as 25, though some enumerators ignored this instruction and just recorded the correct age.
- Occupation, or whether of independent means. This was often abbreviated, so a farm servant may be simply noted as F. S., or a handloom weaver as H.L.W.
- Where born – whether within the county (yes or no), English (E), Irish (I) or Foreign (F).

Unlike subsequent records, no relationships are noted between different members in a household, so don't necessarily assume that wee Annie aged 5 was the daughter of William aged 30 – she could very well be a niece, or even completely unrelated.

NB: 1841 is the most incomplete of all the censuses. Fourteen districts in Fife are missing, as well as a scattering of missing information from other areas in Morayshire, Banffshire, Perthshire, Argyllshire, Buteshire, Ayrshire, Selkirkshire, Roxburghshire and Kirkcudbrightshire. The affected distracts are listed at **www.scotlandspeople. gov.uk/content/help/index.aspx?r=554&1286**.

1851 Census

This was recorded on the night of March 30th 1851, and was much more useful in that it now identified the parish of birth for the individual recorded and also relationships within a household. In addition the boundary information for the area enumerated was more detailed, as were the requirements for the house of the person being listed. It was also the first to ask for medical details. Within an entry are found:

- Boundary location – parish, quoad sacra parish, parliamentary burgh, royalburgh, town or village
- Schedule number
- Name of street, place or road, and name or number of house
- Name and surname of each person enumerated in the house on the night of March 30th
- Relation to head of family
- Condition as to marriage
- Age
- Rank, profession or occupation
- Where born
- Whether blind, deaf or dumb

Records for the Angus registration districts of Careston, Cortachy and Clova, Coupar Angus, Craig and Dun are currently unavailable, as are those for Kilmarnock in Ayrshire, and Strachan in Kincardineshire.

1861 Census

This was recorded on the night of April 7th 1861, and was the first census to be carried out under the authority of the Registrar General for Scotland. It followed the 1851 format but also asked for the following information:

- Number of children attending school between the ages of 5 and 15
- Number of rooms with one or more windows

1871 Census

This was recorded on the night of April 2nd 1871. The boundary details at the top of the page are slightly expanded as follows:

- Civil parish, quoad sacra parish, parliamentary burgh, royal burgh, police burgh, town, village or hamlet

The following was also revised or added:

- Whether deaf and dumb, blind, an imbecile or idiot, or a lunatic
- Number of children attending school between the ages of 5 and 15
- Number of rooms in the property with one or more windows

Tips: *Boundaries*

The areas of geographic administration in Scotland have varied over the centuries. In earliest times these have included the feudal 'baronies', through which a landowner would look after an area on behalf of the king and administer justice on his behalf (the equivalent of an English 'manor'), the 'burghs', administrative centres given the right to trade and to raise their own taxes by the monarch, and the various parish types such as the ecclesiastical 'quoad sacra' parish, and the administrative 'quoad civilia' parishes of the state.

The nature of these administrative borders, particularly with the changing county boundaries down the years (which actually ceased to exist in 1975), can be confusing, but a useful website to help you understand how they have changed down the years is *A Vision of Britain Through Time*, located at **www.visionofbritain.org.uk.**

1881 Census

The 1881 census was recorded on the night of April 3rd. The question about the number of children at school was removed, and the boundary information at the top of the enumerator's return was again expanded:

- Civil parish, quoad sacra parish, school board district, parliamentary burgh, royal burgh, police burgh, town, village or hamlet

The records for books 13-27 for the Dumfriesshire district of Dumfries and the district of Dunscore are missing.

1891 Census

This was recorded on the night of April 5th 1891. In addition to the information previously required, the boundary information was again expanded with further options to record the names of the parliamentary division, municipal burgh, burgh ward and the name of an island.

In addition, the following new information was also required:

- Whether an employer, worker, or working on own account
- Whether able to speak Scottish Gaelic (Gàidhlig), or Scottish Gaelic and English

1901 Census

This census was recorded on the night of March 31st 1901. The boundary information now included the name of the police burgh, and a further question was added, asking whether a worker was working at home. The medical question no longer asked if someone was an 'idiot', instead it asked if they were 'feeble-minded'.

1911 Census

This was recorded April 2nd 1911, and will be released in 2011. Unlike the previous censuses, the original household schedules have survived.

Tip:
It is extremely common to find a woman in a Scottish census reverting to her maiden name after being widowed, and not at all unusual to find her listed under this even when her husband was still living.

Accessing the census

There are three main online sources for Scottish censuses research:

ScotlandsPeople
www.scotlandspeople.gov.uk

The only site to offer access to the digitised entries for the documents is the ScotlandsPeople website (see Chapter 2), which carries all surviving records from 1841 to 1901. Thirty credits cost £6, with a search costing a single credit and the view of the original record a further five. The exception to this is the 1881 census. Originally a transcription of the 1881 census made by the Church of Jesus Christ of the Latter Day Saints was hosted on the site without the original images, with each transcription costing just one credit. When the digitised pages finally went online in early 2009 they were made accessible on the same basis as the other censuses, but the Mormon transcriptions were also retained, and at the original rate. This means that there are two alternative ways to view this census.

The censuses are searchable by name and surname, a second person's forename

The ScotlandsPeople site allows two search methods for the 1881 census.

within a household, sex, age, county and district. The 1881 (LDS) index can also be searched by address and birthplace, though not by a second person's forename. The ScotlandsPeople Centre website does not offer access to the 1881 LDS screen.

Ancestry
www.ancestry.co.uk

Ancestry has provided a series of transcriptions for the 1841 to 1901 Scottish censuses online, but unlike the equivalents on the site for England and Wales it does not provide access to digitised copies of the original images. The records are available through a subscription package or by pay per view. The advantage of the Ancestry version is that it has considerably more fields within which you can perform a search. For 1851-1901 these are:

- First name and surnames
- Residence – county, civil parish, town, address, parish number
- Personal – gender, relationship to head of household, birth year (with +/- ranges), birthplace, occupation
- Family members – father's, mother's and/or spouse's first name
- Other – page number and keywords

The 1841 census has slightly reduced search fields, owing to fact that it was a much more basic document. There are also options to do an 'exact search' or to use wildcards.

In theory, these extra fields make it much easier to locate somebody, particularly if you know when and where they were born. However, a problem that the site suffers from is a very high rate of transcription errors, sometimes quite bizarrely. In one record I once discovered a 'linen weaver' recorded as a 'somam weaver'! Thankfully Ancestry has added a facility to allow users to submit corrections to any entry that is found with a perceived problem. The original entry is not removed, but the correction added – a wise move as the person submitting the correction may in fact be equally wrong.

Freecen
www.freecen.org.uk

A third option for accessing census returns is through the magnificent FreeCEN website. A volunteer project initiated in 1999, it aims to fully transcribe all the British census returns from 1841 to 1891. It is however a project that is taking a very long time to realise, though in many ways this is to its advantage. There are no commercial pressures to get the material online, allowing perhaps the most exhaustive quality control for every entry transcribed. Each county has a co-ordinator, who delegates the census entries out

FreeCEN is always worth checking first.

to volunteers. When the transcriptions are completed and returned, they are repeatedly checked at many different levels for any errors, before being made available online.

For Scotland, the 1841, 1851 and 1861 censuses are those that are being worked on initially, with 1841 having the better coverage at the time of writing. This differs for coverage of England and Wales, with the site favouring the later censuses of 1891 and 1901. A list of what has been recorded so far is available in the *Information About Coverage* section on the site. The returns can be searched as follows:

- Year
- Piece number and enumeration district
- Surname (with option for a phonetic search), and first name
- Marital status
- Age or birth year (with +/- range)
- Sex
- Occupation
- Language (for English and Welsh censuses at present)
- Whether disabled
- Folio, page and schedule numbers
- Street, ecclesiastical districts, civil parish, census place and county
- Birth place and county

The project is always looking for volunteers, and if you are interested, the county co-ordinators details can be found at **www.freecen.org.uk/project.htm**.

Tip: Check all the databases

If you cannot find an entry on one website, it is important to check the others, as sometimes transcription errors can creep in, or results be overlooked. I was once asked to find ancestors for a gentleman listed in the 1851 census by the surname of CLERIHEW, who lived in Aberdeen but claimed to have been born in the parish of Oyne. No evidence of anyone with that name had been found to have been born or married in the parish, or within the censuses. ScotlandsPeople and Ancestry had been tried, but with no results. When I took a look, I also did the search on FreeCEN, and discovered a 60 year old agricultural labourer called 'Earnest CLERYHUGH' in the 1841 census for Oyne. which was then verified by a look at the microfilm roll for the same census. He was subsequently found on Ancestry as 'Ernest CLERGHUGH', a transcription error. This showed that it was unwise to discount the claim of a birthplace as being at Oyne.

Census records at other locations

There are many locally based census transcription projects, some of which have some nice additional features. The best I have come across to date is that of genealogists Graham and Emma Maxwell, located at **www.maxwellancestry.com/census**, which covers several of the Borders counties from 1841-1861. The couple are attempting to link households between the censuses, and also to connect locations listed in the census to digitised maps at the National Library of Scotland website.

Whilst the digitised version of the census records is available at the ScotlandsPeople Centre in Edinburgh, in a minority of cases an image may be difficult to make out, and so the centre also has a complete set of census material on microfilm. Most family history societies have copies of their local censuses on microfilm, and prior to the records being made available online, spent a considerable amount of effort indexing the records, both by first names and surnames, as well as by street names. Many local libraries also hold microfilm copies of both the censuses and the printed indexes.

Earlier censuses

Whilst the census recorded personal information from 1841 onwards, the first enumeration was in fact carried out in 1801, on a purely statistical basis. However, in some parishes the local ministers collated names of heads of households for these earlier censuses, and a few of these lists have survived within kirk session papers and other sources. In addition, many records survive of local censuses gathered for other purposes, including church communion rolls and militia ballot lists.

It is always worth checking with your local county record office for such resources, as well as gateway websites such as GENUKI and Cyndi's List (see Chapter 12). Some material has also been transcribed and/or digitised and made available online – a complete transcript of the 1821 census for the Orkney islands of Deerness, Orphir, St. Andrews, Sandwick, South Ronaldsay & Burray, and Stromness is just one example, available at **www.southronaldsay.net**. *Local Census Listings 1522-1930: Holdings in the British Isles (3rd ed.) by* Jeremy Gibson and Mervyn Medlycott, published by the Federation of Family History Societies, also details some pre-1841 census holdings for Scotland.

Census substitutes

(i) Electoral rolls

Very few people in Scotland had the right to vote prior to 1832, but throughout the 19th Century and early 20th century a series of reforms gradually expanded the electorate, following the struggles of groups such as the Chartists and the Suffragettes.

Within the burghs, a local council would be drawn from members of the Merchant Guild and the trade incorporations. To vote within these elections you had to have a burgess ticket (see Chapter 8). The burgh councils in turn would choose their representative to attend Parliament. In the counties, the right to vote was held only by freeholders who held property worth a certain value, and lists of those entitled to vote might be found within sheriff court records at the NAS.

The various Reform Acts of 1832, 1868 and 1884 slowly increased the male electorate to some sixty per cent of the population, but women remained largely without the franchise. In 1882, unmarried women gained the right to vote in burgh elections, as did married women not living with their families, but it would not be until 1918 that all men over 21 and all women over 30 could vote. In 1930, everybody over 21 gained the right, with the age reduced to 18 in 1971.

Prior to 1868, the results of elections were recorded in a poll book. The details within these vary from parish to parish, but they usually named the voter, his residence, the land qualification for him being allowed to vote, and the name of the candidate for whom he had cast his ballot. Some poll books are held at the NAS and at the NLS but many are held locally in other archives.

Electoral registers from 1872 will alphabetically list the voters' names, addresses and their qualifications to vote, but by 1918, with the electorate having been substantially expanded, the format had to change due to the sheer numbers of people being recorded. From this year the registers therefore list the names of voters by electoral ward. This makes them harder to search for an ancestor if you do not know where they lived, but fortunately trade directories from the period may be able to help with some of the larger cities such as Glasgow (see page 58).

Sometimes people moved quite frequently between addresses, and can therefore be hard to find, but very often they remained within the same area. If the desired record is not found immediately, spend a few more minutes searching the neighbouring streets within the same or adjoining wards. Registers exists in many locations, with substantial collections at the NAS (mainly for the 19th century), the NLS, and in local county libraries, with records prior to 1918 containing evidence of the right to vote in the form of the voter's occupation or property qualification. The NLS has virtually all rolls from 1946 onwards. A useful guide to the locations of burgess rolls, electoral rolls and valuation rolls is *Electoral Registers 1832-1948; and Burgess Rolls* by Jeremy Gibson (2008, The Family History Partnership).

Electoral Intimidation

When the vote was extended in 1832, many landowners tried to bully their tenants into voting for their candidate of choice. The following article from the Scotsman of July 12th 1887 recalls an incident in the general election of 1835:

Coercion, Eviction, And Election Incidents In Perthshire Fifty Years Ago

An 'Old Radical' writes:- When so much is being spoken and written about coercion and eviction at present, perhaps these old episodes may be worthy of notice. They took place on the Murthly estate, in Perthshire, at the time of the general election in 1835. At this time Sir John Stewart, eldest brother of Sir Douglas and of the late Sr W. D. Stewart, was laird, but was an invalid, and quite unable to take any charge of his affairs. So his wife, Lady Jane as she was called, who was a virulent Tory, seized hold of the management of the estates. During the election campaign she galloped about on a horse - always accompanied by three or four gentlemen, also on horseback - over the estates, endeavouring to coerce the tenants into voting for Sir George Murray, the Tory candidate. She probably, by her threats and blandishments, prevented some weak-kneed Liberals from voting for Fox Maule, the Liberal candidate, but there was a considerable number, who dared to call their souls their own, that voted for Mr Maule, as their consciences dictated; but those of them who were yearly tenants, and those whose leases ran out during the currency of this petticoat government, were ruthlessly evicted.

(ii) Directories

Like electoral rolls, directories can be a useful resource for tracing people a year at a time. When a person is no longer recorded within them, it may indicate a possible period where the subject concerned had died or moved away from the vicinity. Edinburgh's first directory did not appear until 1773, and Glasgow's first edition was not published until 1783 – the latter has been digitised and made available at **http://glasgowstories.com/first-glasgow-directory**. Most major libraries will carry a run of volumes for their local area.

Information within directories was organised in several different ways, with people recorded alphabetically by surname, by their trade, and in a section listing streets alphabetically with their associated tenants. The fact that the same information was so recorded can be extremely useful for research

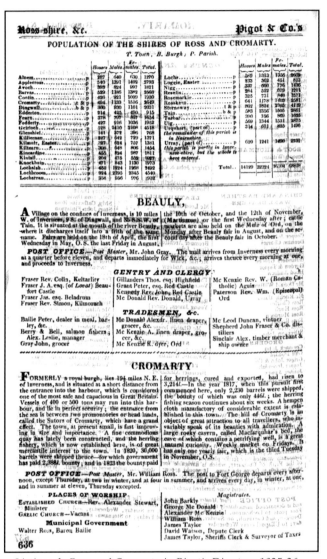

Listings for Ross and Cromarty in Pigot's Directory 1825-26.

purposes. If your ancestor was a grocer, for example, and was listed in a directory in 1838 at a particular address, but cannot be found there in the following edition a year later, you can turn to the section listing people by trade and try to find him listed under the grocers section, which may note a new address for him. In later volumes, the address section may also record the electoral wards which individual streets belonged to, making them a useful companion source for electoral register research. The names of streets with which they intersected may also be listed, which can be useful if trying to locate a street which was subsequently renamed or demolished.

If your ancestor was not from the wealthiest landowning or merchant classes, and was perhaps instead an agricultural labourer or a miner, the chances of him being recorded in the earlier directories are virtually nonexistent, but the books can still provide some useful contextual information for the area within which he resided, such as the names of the local farms or mines which may have employed him. By the end of the century even those on the most modest means began to find themselves included, except for the very poorest in society.

The 1837 *Pigot and Co.'s National Commercial Directory of the Whole of Scotland and of the Isle of Man* is freely available through Google Books (**http://books.google.com**). Ancestry (**www.ancestry.co.uk**) has a few directories online within its *UK City and County Directories 1600-1900* collection. These are *Pigot's Directories for Scotland 1825/1826*, an 1870 *Post Office Directory for Glasgow* and a 1925 *Post Office Directory for Aberdeen*.

In addition, Ancestry also hosts a database entitled *UK and US Directories 1680-1930* which contains extracts from various sources such as trade directories, Scottish book subscription lists up to 1800, vital records announcements from the Gentleman's Magazine and the Scots Magazine, and more. Whilst another useful online resource is Ancestry's *British Phone Books Collection 1880-1984*, which includes listings for Scotland.

Some genealogical supplies retailers also sell CDs of digitised directories, for example, JiGrah Resources has several directories for Glasgow, Edinburgh, Aberdeen, Dundee and Kilmarnock for sale at **www.jigrah.co.uk/mailord/mocdsco.htm**. In addition, the Scottish Genealogy Society has several directories on both CD and microfiche for Edinburgh and Leith.

Further Reading

GIBSON, Jeremy, and MEDLYCOTT, Mervyn (2001) *Local Census Listings 1522-1930: Holdings in the British Isles (3rd ed.)*. Bury: Federation of Family History Societies.
GIBSON, Jeremy (2008). *Electoral Registers 1832-1948; and Burgess Rolls*. Bury: The Family History Partnership.

Stop press: 1939 National Registration

On Friday September 29th 1939 an emergency population census was instituted for the purposes of creating a national identity register. Just as this was book was going to print, the Registrar General for Scotland announced that the Scottish returns can now be obtained for people who were enumerated and who have since been deceased. The information returned is for an individual, not a household, and contains an address, surname and other names, whether male or female, birth (day, month and year), single, married widowed or divorced, and personal occupation. Extracts can be ordered at a cost of £13 each from Extract Services, General Register Office for Scotland, New Register House, 3 West Register Street, Edinburgh, EH1 3YT (cheques payable to the General Register Office for Scotland). A date of death only will need to be supplied.

7. Wills, inventories and confirmations

There are many records that can help us to determine when and how our ancestors died, but in terms of telling us how they once lived, what they owned and who they favoured amongst their friends and family, a useful document to locate is a will and/or inventory of the deceased's possessions. There were two forms of estate that an ancestor may have left behind. The first concerned the personal possessions of the deceased, such as clothing, money, livestock etc, and was known as 'moveable' estate. This could be bequeathed in a will. The second concerned the physical property and land that had been owned by the deceased, and was known as 'heritable' estate. This could not be bequeathed in a Scottish will until 1868, a very significant difference to the English system.

Moveable property
After death, for the deceased's moveable estate to be legally conveyed to his or her heirs, it had to be subjected to a court process known as 'confirmation' (the 'probate' process in the rest of the UK). Until 1823, wills were confirmed in one of the country's many commissary courts, with each area of jurisdiction, known as a 'commissariot', based on the areas previously administered to by the pre-Reformation (i.e. pre-1560) Roman Catholic consistorial courts. The commissary courts were civil courts, thereby differing from the English system, where wills were confirmed until 1858 within ecclesiastical courts. Edinburgh had the most important commissary court, not only dealing with its own parishes, but also with the wills of people who had property in more than one commissariat area, or who lived abroad. From 1823 to 1830 this role was gradually transferred to the Sheriff Courts.

If the deceased left a will, he or she was said to have died 'testate', and the record of confirmation will be known as a 'testament testamentar'. This will include the deceased's date of death, a copy of the will, an inventory of his possessions, and details of the confirmation process. If it is worth noting that prior to the Married Woman's Property Act of 1882, married women could not leave a will, only spinsters and widows, as after marriage any estate a woman may previously have owned was deemed to belong to her husband. The documents employ quite a few archaic Scots legal terms – a deceased John Smith will often be referred to as 'umquhile John Smith', for example, with 'umquhile' meaning 'deceased', and his widow referred to as his 'relict'.

Not all moveable property was conveyable through a will. When a man died, his spouse was automatically entitled to a third of his possessions (the widow's part or 'jus relictae'), his children another third (the bairns' part, or 'legitim'), and only the final third could be bequeathed as he saw fit (the deid's part). As the eldest son usually got to inherit the property, he was not entitled to a share of the legitim, though could be entitled to anything bequeathed by the deceased through the deid's part.

If no will was left, a person was said to have died 'intestate'. In such an instance a

Edinburgh held the highest commissary court in the land prior to 1823.

court may have appointed an executor on behalf of the deceased, and documentation for this may exist in the form of a 'testament dative', similar to what is known in the rest of the UK as a 'letter of administration'. This will again include an inventory of the person's possession, and details of final confirmation.

Other documents

Occasionally a will may be located in the Register of Deeds kept by one of various types of Scottish court (see Chapter 8). It should be remembered that where such a will is located, it does not necessarily mean that its conditions were adhered to if it did not go through the confirmation process.

From the early 19th Century your forebear may also have created a Trust Disposition and Deed of Settlement. This was a way of creating a trust which would allow the owner to convey heritable property to whomever he liked, in much the same way that in England a will could be used from medieval times to bypass the rules of primogeniture. The property was nominally assigned to his trustees, though whilst the deceased was still alive he retained control over it. After death, the trustees would then dispose of the estate according to his wishes.

There were circumstances where a person may have left a will, but decided to alter its conditions at a later stage. These changes were issued in the form of a 'codicil'. If one exists, it is as important to consult this as it is the original will.

It is also worth knowing that not all families went through the courts to sort out moveable estate. Often a family would resolve how to dispose of the deceased's estate themselves.

Looking for wills

All Scottish testaments between 1513 and 1901 have been digitised (over 611,000), and made available to view at **www.scotlandspeople.gov.uk**. The cost to download a will

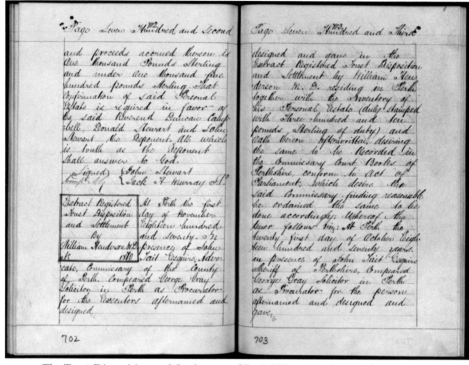

The Trust Disposition and Settlement of Dr. William Henderson of Perth, 1870

is a flat £5 fee per document, no matter how many pages it may contain (though you will often find wills, inventories, codicils etc listed as separate documents), and there is a free index. They can also be viewed at the ScotlandsPeople Centre, and at the NAS, free of charge, though it can be more expensive to print out a will at these two centres.

Following the Sheriff Courts (Scotland) Act of 1876, a series of books was published annually by the commissary clerk in Edinburgh from 1877 to 1959, known as *Calendars of Confirmations and Inventories*. The books contain basic summaries of all confirmations to have been made in Scotland in each year, and are indexed by the name of the deceased, with women indexed under their married names. They record the deceased's name, date and place of death, whether they died testate or intestate, the value of their estate, the date on which confirmation was made, and at which sheriff court. From 1921 there were two volumes a year, the first containing entries for all surnames beginning with the letters A to L, the second from M to Z.

The following is the entry in a 1919 calendar for my great grandfather:

PATON, David Hepburn, Shop manager to R & J Dick Ltd, late of Rue St. Catherine, Brussels, Belgium, formerly of 100 Cumberland Street, Glasgow, died 12 March 1916 at Brussels, intestate. Confirmation granted at Glasgow, 25 February, to Jessie McFarlane or Paton, 18 Aitken Street, Dennistoun, Glasgow, Executrix dative qua relict. Value of estate £204 17s 1d.

In this instance David died without a will, and his personal estate was not transferred until three years after his death, mainly because his wife and family had remained trapped in occupied Brussels for the rest of the war. Many local records offices and libraries have copies of these Calendars, and they can also be consulted at the NAS (General Register House). In addition, the LDS Church has photographed the volumes from 1877 to 1936, which can be ordered up on microfilm to view at your local family history centre (see Chapter 5).

From 1960 to 1984 a microfiche card index can be consulted at the NAS, and the original documents then consulted, whilst from 1985 the records are indexed by computer. The most recent wills for the last ten years are still retained at the relevant sheriff courts – to access these you will need to write to the Commissary Department, Edinburgh Sheriff Court, 27 Chambers Street, Edinburgh, EH1 1LB.

Databases summarising the Registers of Testaments for Edinburgh, Inverness, Hamilton and Campsie can be found at **www.scotsfind.org/databases_free/freedata baseindex.htm**, whilst Ancestry.co.uk also has databases for Aberdeen, Ayrshire, Banffshire, Caithness, Clackmannanshire, Dumfriesshire, Dunbartonshire and Perthshire.

Tip: Outside Scotland
If you have a relative who emigrated, it is still worth checking the Scottish wills and inventories to see if they had any estate in Scotland still within their possession. Often these will yield useful information about their subsequent lives overseas, in addition to their assets in their home country. There may even be a copy of a will made in the adopted country which covered the deceased's wishes regarding his or her estate.

Heritable Property

The other form of personal estate to be dealt with after death was heritable property. Until 1964, the law of primogeniture meant that the eldest son usually inherited his parents' land and any properties thereon, though from 1868 this could be bequeathed in a will to other members of the family. In order for an heir to inherit, however, he or she had to have that right legally confirmed through the Services of Heirs process. This basically meant that a prospective heir went before a jury of local landowners to have his or her right confirmed. The jury would deliberate on the matter and then return or 'retour' its findings to the Royal Chancery in Edinburgh.

The recorded retours were in Latin until 1847, with the exception of the period 1652 to 1657 (Cromwell's Commonwealth period). Records for 1530 to 1699 were summarised in the *Inquisitionum ad Capellam Regis Retornatarum Abbreviatio*, an index for which can be consulted at the NAS (within the General Register House search room), or on a CD produced by the Scottish Genealogy Society. From 1700 you need to consult the *Indexes to the Services of Heirs* at the NAS. Again, the index from 1700 to 1859 is available on CD.

Once an heir had been confirmed legally, they then had the right to inherit. In truth however, many people put off going through the process for years and took possession of the property in question straight away. It was only when they then wanted to sell the property at a later stage that they would suddenly have a panic about getting the paper work sorted. In other cases, the process took years because of legal challenges to the heir's right to inherit. As such, the record can often be found years or even decades after you might expect to find it.

Register of Tailzies

Sometimes within the retours you might come across mention of the words 'taillie' or 'tailzie'. A landowner could actually dictate the course of his land's disposal long after his death by creating a deed called a tailzie, through which he could lay down a series of conditions that had to be adhered to. The breach of such conditions could actually force his successor to give up the land altogether. Tailzies can be extremely useful in identifying entire families, as they would list the name of the person to whom the land should go upon the death of the present incumbent, but also suggest alternative lines should that person die.

A good example of a tailzie is one from the late 18th Century drawn up by Thomas, Earl of Kinnoull. Prior to his death, the good earl had registered his wishes on 18th June 1774 within the Particular Register of Tailzies concerning the disposal of an area of land called Saint Michael's Croft, in the burgh of Perth. In the document he had outlined that the land should in the first instance go to 'all male heirs of his body'. If he had no direct heirs, then it should instead be conveyed to his brother, Doctor Robert Hay Drummond, late Archbishop of York, second lawful son to their father George Earl of Kinnoull, and then to his lawful male heirs. Failing him, it was to go to Mr Edward Hay, youngest brother of Thomas, and his lawful male heirs; and failing that to any other heirs produced by Thomas. If there were no men able to inherit at all, then next up was Thomas' sister Lady Elizabeth Hay, and her heirs, followed by Lady Ann Hay, his second sister, and her heirs, and so on for many more pages…!

Often within a tailzie, if the line of inheritance should fall onto a daughter or other female member of the family, a condition would be set whereby she could only inherit the land if she first married somebody with the same surname as the creator of the tailzie, or somebody who would be willing to take on that name. In addition, that husband would also have to assume the set of Arms inherited by his wife, and in effect legally become a member of that family as if he had done so from birth.

Such arrangements were recorded in the Register of Tailzies from 1688, which is located at the NAS under accession number RT1. An index for this exists, catalogued under RT3/1-3, which can be ordered up for consultation at the Historical Search Room in General Register House. Land could be removed from a tailzie, or 'disentailed', from 1848 onwards, the details of which are also included in the register.

Further Reading

NAS (2009), *Tracing Your Scottish Ancestors –The Official Guide (5th ed.)*. Edinburgh: Birlinn Ltd.
GRANUM, Karen, & TAYLOR, Nigel (2004) *Wills and Other Probate Records*. London: The National Archives.

8. *Where we lived*

Maps

Maps can provide a fascinating insight into how your ancestors' environments have changed over the years, sometimes quite dramatically. They vary in detail and scale, but when considered in chronological order can really bring a story to life for a location. Maps can be found at local records offices, libraries and even in private hands, but in Scotland we are well served online with various resources that can help.

The best source by far is the fantastic National Library of Scotland maps collection at **www.nls.uk/maps/index.html**, with over 20,000 digitised documents. This includes town maps from 1580 onwards, Timothy Pont's maps from the late 16th Century and Ordnance Survey maps from the mid 19th to early 20th centuries. The latter can also be overlaid with a modern street map application from Google Maps (**http://maps.google.co.uk**), to highlight how areas have changed over time. Other useful sources include Lewis's 1840 map of the country at the MAPCO (Map and Plan Collection Online) website, located at **http://archivemaps.com/mapco/scotland/fullmap.htm**, as well as early Ordnance Survey maps located at both **www.oldmaps.co.uk** and the *A Vision of Britain Through Time* website at **www.visionofbritain.org.uk/maps**.

The Royal Commission on the Ancient and Historical Monuments of Scotland website at **www.rcahms.gov.uk** contains the equally useful Canmap service, a map interface that allows you to search for historic sites, and the Canmore database, which provides all sorts of information on properties, including some old photos and diagrams.

A website with an integrated social networking facility is Ancestral Atlas (**www.ancestralatlas.com**). This allows you to view events which happened within a particular area by looking at 'tags' that have been placed at various locations by users of the site, each of which contains a 'wiki' entry. If, for example, you find a note stating that an individual with your surname was born at the house of one of your forebears, you can then e-mail the person who left the tag and compare your research notes. Basic membership for the service is free.

Gazetteers

Gazetteers are books containing detailed information about parishes, towns and villages across the country. The most widely consulted is Frances H. Groome's six volume Ordnance Survey Gazetteer. As well as being available in many libraries, it is also freely online at many websites, including **www.gazetteerofscotland.org.uk** (2nd edition 1896) and the Electric Scotland website at **www.electricscotland.com/history/gazetteer**.

Again, the *A Vision of Britain Through Time* site is extremely useful as it reprints entries from Groome's first edition as well as John Bartholomew's *Gazetteer of the British Isles* from 1887. The site also hosts many different statistics and facts about an area, much of which is derived from analyses of the censuses. Samuel Lewis' *Topographical*

A map showing Perth from 1774.

Dictionary of Scotland from 1846 is another source well worth consulting, and is located online at **www.british-history.ac.uk/source.aspx?pubid=308**.

The *ScotlandsPlaces* website at **www.scotlandsplaces.gov.uk**, is a collaboration between the NAS and the Royal Commission on the Ancient and Historical Monuments of Scotland. The site acts as a local history equivalent to the *ScotlandsPeople* website, and is gazetteer based, replacing the gazetteer currently available through the Scottish Archive Network's *Knowledge Base* website at **www.scan.org.uk/knowledgebase/ search/gazetteer_indexnew.asp**. It provides access to images of maps and plans held by both the RCAHMS and the NAS, as well as some text based sources. These include the 1797 Farm Horse Tax rolls for each county, a list of Owners of Lands and Heritages for Scotland from the early 1870s and the Medical Officers of Health reports from 1891. Searches are performed by clicking on the desired county on a map located on the home page, which can then be narrowed down to individual parishes. Searches can also be performed by a 'search box' which employs a new ScotlandsPlaces gazetteer which holds the place names, descriptions, related places, coordinates, dates and more.

The Statistical Accounts of Scotland

Some of the most useful guides to the various parishes around Scotland are the Statistical Accounts. The Old Statistical Account was drawn up under the direction of Sir

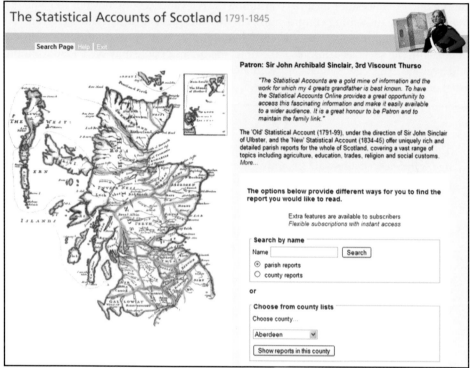

The EDINA website hosts the Old and New Statistical Accounts of Scotland.

John Sinclair of Ulbster between 1791 and 1799, with the New Statistical Account drawn up under the auspices of the Church of Scotland's General Assembly between 1834 and 1845. A third account also exists, created between 1951 and 1992. These can be consulted in many libraries and at the NAS, but the first two series have been digitised and made available to view by the University of Edinburgh at **www.edina.ac.uk/stat-acc-scot**, as well as by Google Books at **http://books.google.com**, where they can be further searched by keyword. This latter edition can also be accessed through the Electric Scotland website at **www.electricscotland.com/HISTORY/statistical/oldndx.htm** (Old Account) and **www.electricscotland.com/HISTORY/statistical/index.htm** (New Account), where the individual volumes can be downloaded in PDF format.

Each volume contains detailed accounts of various parishes across the country. The first series is not arranged in any particular order, so starts with Jedburgh in Roxburghshire, Holywood in Dumfriesshire, Portpatrick in Wigtonshire, etc, for a total of 54 parishes. The second series is based on parishes arranged by county, so Volume 1 deals with Edinburghshire (Midlothian), Volume 2 with Linlithgowshire (West Lothian), Haddingtonshire (East Lothian) and Berwickshire, and so on. The accounts in both series record the topography of an area, its history, and interesting points of antiquity etc, but from our point of view they also give a detailed social portrait of the parish at the time the accounts were written. This can be immensely helpful, for example, if we cannot find our ancestor's birth, as consulting the relevant account may tell you whether there were any dissenting congregations in the same parish, which can then lead you to look for the appropriate records elsewhere. The accounts also provide a great deal of detail on the social conditions of the time, the prices people may have paid for food, and average wages etc, which can really help to provide us with an understanding of what our ancestors' lives were truly like.

The Clearances

The Highland Clearances, known in Gaelic as 'Na Fudaichean' ('the Expulsions'), is one of the most emotive subjects within Scottish history. During the 18th and 19th centuries, thousands of Highlanders (and also tenants in some Lowland areas) were evicted from their homes to make way for sheep, deemed by their landlords to be much more profitable. Many were forced to move to the coast or to the cities of the Central Belt in Scotland, or to emigrate overseas to Canada, the United States and Australia.

The most famous book recalling the events is John Prebble's *The Highland Clearances* (Secker & Warburg, 1963). Another useful book, entitled *The Clergy and the Clearances: the Church and the Highland Crisis 1790-1850*, written by David Paton, was published in 2006 by John Donald Ltd (an imprint of Birlinn). Useful websites recalling the experiences of many who left include www.theclearances.org.

Land transfer records

Records of Scottish land ownership and conveyance are poorly served by the internet, and require a bit of digging at an archive. In Scotland, land was exchanged via the laws of feudalism right up to the year 2004, when the Abolition of Feudal Tenure etc. (Scotland) Act 2000 came into force, finally ridding the country of a system which had been abandoned in England and Wales during the Middle Ages.

Feudalism basically concerned a series of relationships between dominant 'superiors' and their subordinate 'vassals', with the monarch the highest superior in the land, holding Scotland on behalf of God. To manage the land, large tracts were carved up into parcels of land known as 'feus' and then passed on to various high ranking nobles or institutions, who were termed 'feuars'. In return, the feuars made an annual or twice yearly payment called a 'feu duty' to the superior, after which they were said to be 'infeft'. These feudal agreements were hereditary, and so the land could be passed on to a feuar's heir after death.

Vassals to the monarch, nobles and institutions could also become superiors themselves by further dividing the land into smaller portions for their own vassals (a process called 'subinfeudation'), making them 'intermediate lawful superiors' or 'subject superiors'. This carried on again and again down a sort of feudal pyramid, to the level of merchants and lesser nobles with much smaller holdings. Any feuar could build on the land with their immediate superior's consent, and could rent out their properties, but if the superior imposed any restrictions these had to be adhered to, otherwise the land could undergo 'reversion', in other words be taken back by the superior.

The only real exceptions to this method of land holding concerned land owned by the Church, which was held under what was termed 'allodial' 'odal' or 'udal' tenure, basically outright ownership. A similar system operated in the Orkney and Shetland islands, and still exists there to this day, to the great pride of the islanders! A useful article on udal tenure, which has particular ramifications for the ownership of the shoreline on the islands, is available at **www.pandius.com/udallaw.html**.

Tip: Term days and quarter days

There were two 'term days' every year – Whitsun, set at May 15th, and Martinmas, on November 11th – on which rents and feu duties were traditionally paid. Along with Candlemas on February 2nd and Lammas on August 1st, they formed the four 'quarter days', which divided up the legal year and acted as holidays and periods of recruitment for servants and agricultural labourers. From 1886 the dates changed to the 28th of each of the four respective months, where they have since remained.

Charters

Transactions involving property were recorded in charters and writs, which stipulated various agreed conditions between the vassal and the superior, including the amount of feu duty and any penalty conditions for lack of payment on the part of the vassal or a lack of oversight on the part of the superior. Often the records show how a property came into the possession of a person's family prior to it being passed on to an heir, or may show the clauses that lead to a property's income or benefit being bequeathed to a relative in 'liferent', i.e. for the term of his or her natural life, even past the feuar's own death (common in marriage settlements). As such, the records can be extremely desirable to locate.

The documents can exist in many forms. A 'Charter of Feu' was granted upon the original creation of a feu, and was usually reproduced almost word for word in subsequent charters dealing with the same property.

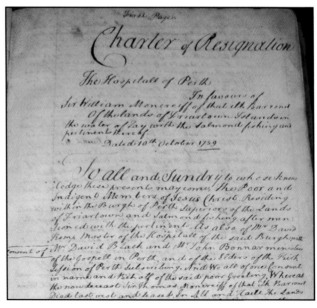

A Charter of Resignation from 1759 in favour of Sir William Moncrieffe of that Ilk.

There were also documents known as 'Precepts of Clare Constat', issued when an heir inherited a property, which established that an applicant was clearly recognised by his or her immediate superior as the lawful heir. If the heir's superior was the Crown, however, they only needed to be confirmed through the Services of Heirs procedure (see Chapter 7). For those lower down the chain, even with a precept of clare constat they could still go through the Services of Heirs procedure, to make it absolutely crystal clear and to have the further backing of law.

If a feuar sold his property to another buyer, a 'Charter of Resignation' was issued, temporarily returning the land to the control of the superior, and a 'Charter of Confirmation' then granted to the new owner to complete the purchase. Finally, a 'Charter of Novodamus' could also be granted, where land was temporarily returned to a superior for a mistake to be corrected or a change made to the document, before being granted back to the vassal.

Charters are held in many locations, and can be loose or bound together in volumes known as 'chartularies'. The NAS holds a *Calendar of Charters* under RH6, which is indexed, and which contains details on charters recorded between 1142 and 1600. A series of legal writs from 1601 to 1830 can also be found under RH7. The archive holds many additional charters within its Gifts and Deposits collections (GD), which can be searched online at **www.nas.gov.uk/onlinecatalogue**.

Elsewhere, the Scottish Archive Network (SCAN) at **www.scan.org.uk** can also be consulted for charters held within local archives, whilst the National Register of Archives for Scotland (NRAS) is another possibility at **www.nas.gov.uk/onlineregister**, for privately held records.

Ancestry (**www.ancestry.co.uk**) has databases for charters granted in the earldoms of Dundonald (1219-1672) and Wigtown (1214-1681), whilst the *Records of the Parliament of Scotland to 1707* site at **www.rps.ac.uk** has a fully searchable database with summaries of various charters for the pre-Union period with England, from 1235 to 1707.

At the end of any charter, a superior would give an instruction for his or her bailies to grant permission for the drawing up of an 'Instrument of Sasine', a legal document to allow the transaction to be recorded in the Register of Sasines, with 'sasine' (pronounced 'sayzin') being the act of taking possession of the land. Whilst original charters may be difficult to locate, the Registers of Sasines are considerably easier to find.

Tip: Scots
Many Scottish legal documents employ archaic forms of wording derived from the Scots language. A useful online glossary to explain some of these terms can be found at http://pagesperso-orange.fr/euroleader/wedderburn/glossaryA-E.htm#A, whilst www.dsl.ac.uk/dsl/index.html hosts the Dictionary of the Scots Language. A Concise Scots Dictionary by Mairi Robinson is also available via Google Books (http://books.google.com), whilst the ScotlandsPeople website has a useful guide at www.scotlandspeople.gov.uk/content/help/index.aspx?r=551&431.

Sasines

Property transactions have been recorded in various Registers of Sasines from as early as 1599 in some counties, though mostly from 1617 onwards. Until 1868 these were recorded in the 'Burgh Registers' for the country's royal burghs (mostly unindexed), in 'Particular Registers' for individual counties across the country; or in a 'General Register' based in Edinburgh, for transactions across most of Scotland (with the exception of the three Lothian counties), including property based across two or more counties. Whilst most registers are today held at the NAS, pre-1809 burgh registers for Glasgow, Aberdeen and Dundee are still held in their respective local city archives, with some particular registers also held locally, which can again be sourced through SCAN (**www.scan.org.uk**).

Digitised abridgements for the particular and general registers from 1781 to 1868 have been made available to view on terminals within the NAS buildings. This can be searched by surname or place name, and will usually give enough information to let you know who granted a piece of land, the name of the recipient, and the arrangement by which it was transferred. However, the original sasine itself can also be ordered up at the Historic Search Room at HM General Register House, and can provide further information such as a description of the land in question – useful for noting the exact boundaries of a property, and some physical details of the house itself.

The following is an example of a sasine abridgement:

MARION McKECHNIE, spouse of Hugh Paton, Grocer, Largs, as heir to John McK-ECHNIE, Grocer and Manufacturer there, her father, Seised, in the half of a Dwelling House with Byre and Yard at the back thereof on the north side of the Street of LARGS, and of a Barn extending to about 10 Feet in length adjoining, par. Largs; on Pr. Cl. Con. by Gen. Sir Thomas Makdougall Brisbane of Makerstoun and Brisbane, Sept. 21. 1849 P. R. 353.249.

"Pr. Cl. Con." is short for "Precept of Clara Constat", the document which showed that Marion was entitled to take over her father's feu from the local feudal superior, Sir Thomas Makdougall Brisbane.

A list of printed indexes for registers prior to 1781 can be consulted online at **www.nas.gov.uk/guides/sasines.asp**. Many of the sasine records can also be ordered up through the LDS catalogue on microfilm and viewed at a Family History Centre, whilst evidence of pre-Union sasines can again be found at **www.rps.ac.uk** for agreements that came within the interest of the original Scottish Parliament.

Registers of Scotland

In 1868 the general register was reorganised into county based divisions, and the particular registers were abolished. An index to entries within this new general register, compiled by place name from 1872, can be consulted at the NAS.

However, from 1979 a programme to slowly phase these registers out has been in operation, with the creation of a new Land Register, maintained by Registers of Scotland (**www.ros.gov.uk**). In the old system, properties were identified within sasines by a physical description of which other properties bordered it in all sides. In the Land Register, they are now pinpointed exactly using the Ordnance Survey Map. From 1870, a series of search sheets has been created for each property listed in the old registers, and the entries for these from 1875 to 1993 have all being digitised and can be consulted at the Registers of Scotland offices in Glasgow or Edinburgh, for a small fee. These search sheets are invaluable, in that they can give long lists of transactions for a property from the present day back to 1875, with details of the relevant sasine abridgements or Land Register entries included.

For properties sold since the year 2000, basic details of transactions are also freely available on websites such as **www.ourproperty.co.uk**, which will name recent applicants and granters for house purchases. Records of planning applications affecting a property can also sometimes be found in the Edinburgh Gazette, available for free at **www.gazettes-online.co.uk**.

Register of Deeds

A deed is essentially an agreement between two individuals which was voluntarily registered in a court to prevent a fraudulent claim, and which could encompass a variety of subjects, from the issuing of bonds (loans) and marriage settlements, to the disposal of land and mortgages (known as 'wadsets'). Various types of Scottish court recorded deeds meaning that they can be located in a number of different locations.

The Court of Session, the supreme civil court in the country, had a Register of Deeds known as the *Books of Council and Session*, which was first started in 1554 in Edinburgh. From 1661 to 1811 all deeds recorded within the register were kept by three separate clerks called Dalrymple, Durie and Mackenzie, and as such the records were initially filed in separate series prefixed with DAL, DUR and MACK (now catalogued as RD2, 3 and 4). From 1811, the records form one series under RD5.

The records are sporadically indexed up to 1770, though annual indices have been compiled from that year onwards, which can be consulted in the Historical Search Room at the NAS's HM General Register House. Prior to 1770, where an index exists, it will name both parties to an agreement, though after this date only the granter makes an appearance.

Registers of deeds were also kept by the lower sheriff courts, and are fairly poorly indexed. A guide on the NAS website, located at **www.nas.gov.uk/guides/deeds.asp**, shows which courts' records are held at the archive, and for which year. The guide also provides information on other courts which kept registers, such as the Royal Burgh Courts and the Commissary Courts. Bear in mind that when a document is registered by a court, it is the date of registration that is indexed, and not the date of the original deed granted, which could be much earlier.

The Courts

The official website for the Scottish courts is www.scotcourts.gov.uk. Both civil and criminal cases in Scotland can be heard in the Sheriff Courts. An appeal in a civil case is heard by the Court of Session, the highest civil court in the land, and any further appeal is then heard by the House of Lords. Civil cases can include sequestration hearings (bankruptcy), accident enquiries, debts cases and much more. The NAS catalogue is a useful first step to locate sheriff court papers for civil cases, and to consult the records themselves you will need to visit West Register House. Records not held at the NAS are those for Lerwick and Kirkwall Sheriff Courts, and those from all other Scottish sheriff courts less then 25 years old.

For criminal matters, the High Court of Justiciary is the supreme criminal court, with Sheriff Courts, District Courts and Justices of the Peace Courts beneath it. All High Court trials from 1800-1994 have been indexed by the NAS, with the index being made available on the catalogue also. Other courts to hold jurisdiction in the past were the barony courts (until 1747), Admiralty Courts (for crimes on the high seas), Burgh Courts and Franchise Courts.

An in depth guide to all Scottish courts and the locations of their records, is available online at www.nas.gov.uk/guides/crime.asp.

Rents and valuations

Feuars could lease out their properties to tenants. Locating such agreements through landowners' estate records, rental rolls, etc., can be done through the catalogues mentioned above, as can various tax records which can help to place people in various properties at various times, though such records can be patchy.

A useful set of records which can be of immense help is the Valuation Rolls from 1855 to 1989, which recorded annual rents worth more than £4 in value, along with the sitting tenants and their occupations, the owners, and any feu duties or payments due. The rolls are held both in local county archives and at the NAS, where a copy was legally required to be deposited, and which can now be consulted on microfilm. The Valuation Roll for Glasgow in 1913-14 can be viewed online at **www.theglasgow-story.com**, with the site also containing electoral ward maps for the period, on which the geographic divisions of the rolls were based. For Dumfriesshire, several rolls from 1896-97 have been digitised and made freely available at **www.maxwellancestry.com/ancestry/resources.htm**. It is expected that in 2010 the *Scotlands-People* website will host digitised versions of the valuation rolls up to 1915-16 for the whole of Scotland, though these will only be indexed for 1855-56 and then for every tenth year thereafter, i.e., 1865-66, 1875-76, etc up to 1915-16.

Another useful online tool is found on the FamilyRelatives subscription based website (**www.familyrelatives.com**), being a *Return of Scottish Landowners* as printed by the House of Lords in 1874. This details the names and addresses of every landowner holding more than one acre in Scotland, and is arranged in counties. It details returns for all those living outside of a burgh containing more than 20,000 individuals, and separately for those living within such a burgh. The records also note how much land was owned, the annual value of the land and the heritage derived from it, with the definition of an owner including feuars, leaseholders of 99 years or more, and liferenters. The returns can also be purchased on CD from S&N Genealogy Supplies Ltd (**www.genealogysupplies.com**), and viewed on the Genealogist website (**www.thegenealogist.co.uk**).

Estate records

Whilst many land records exist which can help you to trace the wealthier in society, estate papers are often the means for finding out about poorer folk and the labouring classes, most usefully for the period before the 1841 census.

In order to identify the landowner for the area within which you are interested, it is worth consulting the Old and New Statistical Accounts (see earlier), which in many cases will list all of the landowners as well as a history of some of the previous owners. Once you know who owned the land, the next job is to then find the records. These can be located absolutely anywhere in Scotland, so may take a bit of digging to turn up.

The NAS holds many records from estates amongst its Gifts and Deposits collection (GD), with particularly good examples including the Breadalbane Muniments (GD112) and the Grandtully Muniments (GD237) for Perthshire, and the Duke of Gordon's papers (GD44) for his Aberdeenshire lands. Other records of use can be found with the RH9 and RH11 series and the CR series (Commissioners of Crown Estates).

The following are examples of rental payments concerning my five times great grandfather Peter Henderson, who lived in the Airntully area of Kinclaven parish in Perthshire:

> *Perth: Rental of the baronies of Strathbraan, Murthly and Airntully dated 1801*
>
> *Peter Henderson crop 1801*
> *Entry 1793*
> *Endurance 19*
> *Expiration 1812*
> *Coals 2 bolls 2 firlots*
> *3 Hens*
> *£18 14s 7d 6*
>
> (Source: NAS CR4/233)

This not only tells me about the rent that Peter had to pay annually, but also that he had a nineteen years lease. (To find out about measures such as 'bolls' and 'firlots', visit the SCAN website's *Weights and Measures* page at **www.scan.org.uk/measures/index.asp**).

Rental records rarely list anybody other than the head of household, but the fact that they can show the presence of an ancestor in the parish at a particular time is still extremely useful.

Other useful records found within estate papers include militia lists. In the late 1790s and early 1800s the threat from Napoleon was at its highest, and landowners drew up their own militias from their tenants. The following is an example of members from the Crerar family found within the militia lists of the Breadalbane Muniments:

> *Ardtallanaig recruits*
>
> *Skiag – Duncan Crerar, son to Donald Crerar crofter, April 1793 (Donald Crerar has got a croft in Skiag)*
>
> (Source: NAS GD 112/52/522)

Beyond the NAS, you may find estate papers held at county records offices, or still in private hands. To locate these you will need to use the SCAN catalogue or that of the National Register of Archives for Scotland. Some records may also be listed through the English equivalent at **www.nationalarchives.gov.uk/nra**.

Taxes

The authorities have spent many years dreaming up ingenious forms of taxation to raise funds for the state, but whilst they may have annoyed our ancestors they can be helpful for us today in locating where they lived and in assessing their financial status. The records are held at the NAS and include returns for the following:

Cart Tax	1785-92	E326
Commutation Tax	1784-98	E326
Dog Tax	1797-98	E326
Hearth Tax	1690	E69
Horse Tax and Farm Horse Tax	1797-98	E326
Income Tax	1799-1802	E326
Poll Tax	1693, 1695 and 1698	E70
Wheel carriage Tax	1785-98	E326
Window Tax	1778-98	E326

Further Reading

NAS (2009), *Tracing Your Scottish Ancestors –The Official Guide (5th ed.)*. Edinburgh: Birlinn Ltd.

GIBB, Andrew Dewar (1946) *Students' Glossary of Scottish Legal Terms*. Edinburgh: W. Green & Son Ltd.

DURIE, B. (2009) *Scottish Genealogy*. Stroud: The History Press.

MENZIES, A., MITFORD, J., and HUNTER, J. (1863). Conveyancing According to the Law of Scotland: Being the Edited Lectures of the Late Allan Menzies. Edinburgh: Bell and Bradfute. Available online at Google Books (**http://books.google.com**)

MURRAY, James (1900) *Life in Scotland A Hundred Years Ago, as Reflected in the Old Statistical Account of Scotland, 1791-99*. Paisley: Alexander Gardner.

9. *Earning a Crust*

To understand what our ancestors did for a living, we start with the descriptions as noted in the statutory and parish records, as well as within the censuses. Some job descriptions may be completely baffling when we first come across them – a useful resource for translating them is the Scots Family website at **www.scotsfamily.com/occupations.htm**.

By taking the entries in all of these records and listing them chronologically, it is possible to note how a career may have developed throughout our ancestors' lives, though it is worth bearing in mind that people sometimes exaggerated their callings in the records. However, for many vocations additional records exist which can greatly add to the family story. For specific reading on many of these trades and occupations, a useful book is *Scottish Trades, Professions, Vital Records and Directories – a Selected Biography* by D. Richard Torrance (1998, SAFHS, 2nd edition).

Military records

At some point in your tree you will almost certainly find somebody who was connected with the military, of which there are currently three main branches, the Army, the Royal Navy and the RAF. Following the Union of 1707 most military records will be found in England, though some may still be found in Scotland, particularly militia records. In addition to the actual records of their attestation to a service, and their records of service, it is also worth checking for pension details and regimental histories. Increasingly a great deal of material is becoming available online for the services in the late 19th and 20th centuries, but considerably more still resides in the archives.

(i) Militias

There have been various militias drawn up in Scotland over the centuries, such as the fencible, volunteer and yeomanry regiments. Their records can often be located in records of both sheriff and county courts, but also within the NAS and the National Archives at Kew.

The Fencibles were drawn up in the 1790s as a sort of home guard, designed to protect their immediate vicinities only, allowing the regular army to go off to fight the Napoleonic French. An ancestor of mine, William Paton, was a member of Breadalbane's Fencibles, a unit first raised by the Earl of Breadalbane in 1793. He joined in 1797, and his attestation papers, held within the regimental papers at the NAS under GD112/52/544 (in the Breadalbane Muniments), provided me with a complete physical description of him. For more on the Fencible Corps, read Ron McGuigan's excellent dissertation on the regiments, which includes a detailed list of units, at **www.napoleonseries.org/military/organization/fencibles/c_fencibles.html**.

In 1797 the Scottish Militia Act was passed, requiring a ballot of men aged between

18 and 30 for compulsory service, with another act in 1802 extending the age limit to 45. Again, many county archives have records of these ballots and of censuses carried out to ascertain who was eligible for service. The following is the wording of a typical enumeration form for Perth based men in 1802:

> TAKE Notice that you are hereby required within Fourteen Days from the Date hereof, to prepare or produce a Lift in Writing, to the best of your Belief, of the Christian and Surname of each and every Man resident in your Dwelling House, from and after the age of Eighteen Years complete, and not exceeding the Age of Forty-five years complete, distinguishing every Person in your Dwelling House of such age as aforesaid, claiming to be exempt from serving in the Militia, together with the Ground of every such Claim delivered to my house at South Street Perth.

The form required those enumerated to list how many dependant children they had, whether they owned property to the value of at least £50, or whether they had any other reason for exemption from service. Failure to fill out the document could result in a penalty payment of ten pounds sterling, though appeals were held and in some cases substitutes took the place for those required to serve.

Records of Scottish militias can be found within sheriff and county court records, and so it is worth checking the holdings for the relevant counties at the NAS. You will also occasionally find estate records which include lists of males eligible to sign up to the militia if called upon to do so (see Chapter 8). The Origins Network (**www.origins network.com**) has a Militia Attestations Index (1886-1910) online in its British Origins section, listing the names of 110,000 recruits drawn from across the British Isles, including many recruits from southern and central Scotland. A further 12,500 British recruits are listed within its Irish Militia Attestations Index (1872-1915), available in the Irish Origins section, all of whom signed up to the Royal Garrison Artillery. Both collections can also be consulted at the World Vital Records website (**www.worldvitalrecords.com**).

(ii) Army

Records for soldiers who fought in Scottish army units before the union with England in 1707 are mainly found within muster rolls held at the NAS under accession number E100, and are arranged by regiment and then companies or troops. Soldiers from all ranks are included, but it is necessary to know which regiment your ancestor was in to find him, though often men joined the unit raised by their local landowner. Estate papers may also shed some light on officers granted commissions to a particular regiment in this period. From 1670 army commissions were recorded in the warrant books for the Secretary of State, which can be sourced through the NAS at SP4. Many of the muster roll records and commissions have been transcribed and indexed by Charles Dalton and are available through two books *The Scots Army 1661-1688* (1909, republished by Greenhill Books, 1989) and *English Army Lists and Commission Registers 1661-1714* (published by Eyre and Spottiswoode, London, 1892-1904, 6 volumes).

Records following the union are by and large kept at the National Archives (TNA) at Kew, though some material is available at regimental museums. A useful online guide to the holdings of the National Archives is available at **www.nationalarchives.gov.uk/militaryhistory/army**, whilst information on relevant museums can be found at the Army Museums Ogilby Trust website at **www.armymuseums. co.uk**.

Prior to the mid 19th century officers tend to be the better recorded members of the army. TNA has a complete set of Army Lists from 1759 onwards in the Microfilm Reading Room at Kew, which give brief details of officers serving in individual regiments. Hart's Army List was an unofficial account of officers published by Lieutenant General Henry Hart in 1839, and produced quarterly thereafter up to 1915. These also give short biographical entries which often include service details for all featured, and are also held at TNA under WO211. Many army lists are beginning to find their way online at **www.familyrelatives.com** (1858), **www.thegenealogist.co.uk** (1806, 1842, 1857, 1863, 1877, 1881, 1904, 1915, 1920, 1938) and **www.findmypast.co.uk** (1798, 1840, 1878, 1888).

For the Napoleonic wars, a Peninsula Medal Roll is available at **www. findmypast.co.uk** covering 1793-1814, listing awards to soldiers of all ranks who fought under the Duke of Wellington. A Waterloo Medal Roll from 1815 is also available through the site, listing some 37,000 recipients from all ranks who fought at the Battle of Waterloo. In addition, a roll call for those who fought at Waterloo is online at **www.familyrelatives.com**, with information mainly on officers but also for some NCOs who later received commissions within the British Army.

My great grandmother's brother, Charles Mackintosh MacFarlane, who fought with both the Cameron and Seaforth Highlanders. in WW1.

For the Boer War, a useful website with information on both those who survived and the casualties is **www.roll-of-honour.com/Databases/BoerDetailed/index.html**. For the Crimean war, a similar site is that of the Crimean War Research Society at **http://cwrs.russianwar.co.uk**.

TNA has several resources available through its Documents Online service (see Chapter 2), which can be downloaded for a fee. For the First World War these include selected regimental war diaries, Women's Army Auxiliary Corps records, campaign medal index cards, and prisoner of war interviews. Other records include Victoria Cross registers from 1856, and recommendations for all honours and awards to British army personnel from 1935 to 1990.

TNA also has a useful set of records under WO97 which record soldiers who became in- or out-pensioners of the Royal Chelsea Hospital. These are for non-officer ranks only and mainly cover the period from 1843-1899, with some additional entries from 1900-1913. They are extremely useful in that they give attestation and discharge records, providing a brief snapshot of the soldier's career. At the time of writing these records are

SHORT SERVICE
Army Form B. 265.

(7 years with the Colors, and 5 years in the Reserve.)

ATTESTATION OF

No. *2498* Name *Charles Mac Farlane* Corps *Cameron Highlanders*

Joined at *Inverness* on *15 May 1891*

Questions to be put to the Recruit before Enlistment.

1. What is your Name? — *Charles Mac-Farlane*
2. In or near what Parish or Town were you born? — In the Parish of *Inverness* near the Town of *Inverness* in the County of *Inverness*
3. Are you a British Subject? — *Yes*
4. What is your Age? — *18* years *—* Months.
5. What is your Trade or Calling? — *Photographer*
6. Have you resided out of your Father's house for three years continuously in the same place, or occupied a house or land of the yearly value of £10 for one year, and paid rates for the same, and, in either case, if so, state where? — *No*

You are hereby warned that if after enlistment it is found that you have given a wilfully false answer to any of the following eight questions, you will be liable to a punishment of two years imprisonment with hard labour.

7. Are you, or have you been, an Apprentice? if so, where? to whom? and for what period? — *Yes Served 3½ years with W. M'naker Inverness (not bound)*
8. Are you Married? — *No*
9. Have you ever been sentenced to Imprisonment by the Civil Power? — *No*
10. Do you now belong to Her Majesty's Army, the Marines, the Militia, the Militia Reserve, the Royal Navy, the Volunteers, the Yeomanry, the Naval Artillery Volunteers, the Army Reserve, or the Naval Reserve Force? If so, to what Corps? — *Yes 1st V. B. Cam: High'ds*
11. Have you ever served in Her Majesty's Army, the Marines, the Militia, the Militia Reserve, or the Royal Navy? If so, state which and cause of discharge — *No*
12. Have you ever been discharged from any part of Her Majesty's Forces, with Ignominy, or as Incorrigible and Worthless, or on account of conviction of felony, or of a sentence of penal servitude, or have you been dismissed with disgrace from the Navy? — *No*
13. Have you truly stated the whole, if any, of your previous Service? — *Yes*
14. Have you ever been rejected as unfit for Her Majesty's Service? If so, on what grounds? — *No*
15. Are you willing to be vaccinated or re-vaccinated? — *Yes*
16. For what Corps are you willing to be enlisted, or are you willing to be enlisted for General Service? — *Cameron Highlanders*
17. Did you receive a Notice, and do you understand its meaning, and who gave it to you? — *Yes (Name Serg't Inst Sanderson) (Corps 1st V. B. Cam: High)*
18. Are you willing to serve upon the following conditions provided Her Majesty should so long require your service?
(a) For the term of Twelve Years, for the first seven years in Army Service and for the remaining five years in the First Class of the Army Reserve, or if, at the termination of such period of Army Service, you are serving beyond the seas, then for the first eight years in Army Service and for the remaining four years in the 1st Class of the Army Reserve.
(b) If, at the expiration of the above-mentioned term of Army Service, whether of seven or eight years, a state of war exists, then, if so directed by the competent Military Authority, to serve in Army Service for a further period not exceeding 12 months.
(c) If, at the expiration of the above-mentioned term of Army Service, you are so required by a proclamation from Her Majesty in case of imminent national danger or great emergency, then to serve in Army Service so as to complete your term of 12 years, and for a further period not exceeding 12 months.
(d) If the above-mentioned term of 12 years expires while you are on service with the Regular Forces beyond the seas, or while a state of war exists with a Foreign Power, or while Soldiers in the Reserve are required by proclamation to continue in or re-enter upon Army Service, then to serve for a further period not exceeding 12 months. — *Yes*

I, *Charles Mac-Farlane* do solemnly declare that the above answers made by me to the above questions are true, and that I am willing to fulfil the engagements made.

Signature of Recruit. *Chas McFarlane* Signature of Witness. *Thomas Hopkins*

OATH TO BE TAKEN BY RECRUIT ON ATTESTATION.

I, *Charles Mac-Farlane* do make Oath, that I will be faithful and bear true Allegiance to Her Majesty, Her Heirs, and Successors, and that I will, as in duty bound, honestly and faithfully defend Her Majesty, Her Heirs, and Successors, in Person, Crown, and Dignity against all enemies, and will observe and obey all orders of Her Majesty, Her Heirs, and Successors, and of the Generals and Officers set over me. So help me God.

Witness my hand. Signature of Recruit *Charles McFarlane*

Signature of Witness *Thomas Hopkins*

CERTIFICATE OF MAGISTRATE OR ATTESTING OFFICER.

The Recruit above-named was cautioned by me that if he made any false answer to any of the above questions he would be liable to be punished as provided in the Army Act.

The above questions were then read to the recruit in my presence.

I have taken care that he understands each question, and that his answer to each question has been duly entered as replied to, and the said recruit has made and signed the declaration and oath before me at *Inverness*

on this *15* day of *May* 1891

Signature of the Justice

The service record of my grandmother's brother, Charles Mackintosh MacFarlane.

The war memorial at Inverary.

being digitised by FindmyPast.co.uk. In the meantime, each soldier listed can be found through a simple keyword search at **www.nationalarchives.gov.uk/catalogue**.

The most useful records for the First World War are those of soldiers' service records. A great many were destroyed during a bombing raid in London in the Second World War, but those that survived have been digitised and made available at **www. ancestry.co.uk**. They are classed in two categories, British Army WW1 Service Records 1914-1920 (from TNA WO363) and British World War 1 Pension Records 1914-1920s (TNA WO364). Also at Ancestry is the WWI Medal Rolls collection, which lists every person who received a medal of some sort for the war, and which is the most complete collection of WW1 records available.

Other online sources for WW1 include the *Soldiers Who Died in the Great War* collection at both FamilyRelatives.com and FindmyPast.co.uk, with both sites also offering other collections such as the *National Roll of the Great War, De Ruvigny's Roll* and others. It is also possible to trace an officer's promotions through the Edinburgh and London Gazette newspapers at **www.gazettes-online.co.uk** – in fact, when an officer's promotion was so recorded, it was ...id that he had been 'gazetted'.

For both world wars, a list of those who died, alongside details of their burial or memorial, is located at the Commonwealth War Graves Commission website at **www.cwgc.org** (also covering RAF and Royal Navy casualties). Two equally useful sites are those of the Scottish War Memorials Project at **www.scottishwarmemorials.com** and the Scottish War Graves Project at **http://scottishwargraves.phpbbweb.com**. Both have recently joined forces to form the Scottish Military Research Group (**www.span-glefish.com/scottishmilitaryresearchgroup**), which has started to release a series of CDs identifying the names of soldiers on war memorials, county by county. A useful site for all historical matters to do with the First World War is *The Long, Long Trail* at **www.1914-1918.net**, with its own dedicated discussion forum at **http://1914-1918.inv sionzone.com/forums**.

Additional records held at the NAS include a list of 31,000 Scottish soldiers' wills, with 26,000 from WW1, and 4700 from WW2. Included are some returns for RAF and Royal Flying Corps men, and the remainder of the collection dates between 1857 and 1966. The records have been digitised but can only be viewed on the computers in the Historical Search Room.

The NAS also has a series of WW1 Military Tribunal Appeal papers held under HH30 concerning conscientious objectors from the Edinburgh, Lothians and Borders regions of Scotland. Sadly these documents are the only such papers still in existence for Scotland, but they are being digitised and made available for view within the building also.

For World War Two, Ancestry has two useful British databases available. The *UK Army Roll of Honour 1939-1945* lists casualties as originally recorded at TNA's War Office: Roll of Honour, Second World War collection at WO 304, which was compiled from various War Office records between 1944 and 1949. The database includes the name of the soldier, birthplace, residence, enlisted rank, rank at the time of death, the enlisted regiment, the regiment at the time of death, the theatre of war or country where the soldier was wounded or died, and the date of death. The *British Army Prisoners of War 1939-1945* collection provides details on over 100,000 British POWs, from all the forces (excluding airmen), including details on name, rank, army number, regiment, POW number, camp type, camp number, camp location, record office and number, and any additional notes.

Tip: Pensioners in the census

If you find a census entry between 1841 and 1901 listing somebody as a 'pensioner' in the occupation box, it will usually refer to a military pension – the basic state pension was not introduced into Scotland until January 1909, and was only payable at that stage to those over the age of 70.

(iii) Royal Air Force

The RAF was formed in 1918 following a merger between the Army Flying Corps and the Royal Naval Air Service. Service records for the Women's Royal Air Force from 1914-1918 are available from TNA's Documents Online service, whilst the facility also provides air combat reports from the Second World War. The *Recommendations for Honours and Awards* list, available on the site, includes awards for members of the RAF.

Also online are a series of RAF lists at **www.familyrelatives.com** for the years 1920, 1922 and 1929, whilst at **www.ancestry.co.uk** there is the *Royal Aero Club Aviators Cer-*

tificates 1914-1950 collection, listing some 28,000 index cards and 34 photo albums of aviators' issued with flying licenses, and which includes many early pilots who flew with the Army, Navy and RAF.

For the Battle of Britain, a useful guide is Kenneth G. Wynn's *Men of the Battle of Britain* (2nd ed. 1999, CCB Associates), a phenomenal work detailing the careers of all those who fought the Luftwaffe over the skies of Britain in 1940, with photos for most pilots and aircrew included. Of equal interest are the two volumes of *Aces High* by Christopher Shores (Grub Street, 1994 and 1999), which provide detailed biographies on the highest scoring British and Commonwealth pilots of the entire war.

A series of 61 wills belonging to officers and men of the RAF from 1939 to 1950 is held at the NAS under SC70/10. The FamilyRelatives.com website also has a database of Royal Air Force Deaths from 1935 to 1950.

If your ancestor was an officer in the RAF Volunteer Reserve during the Second World War, you may find some further biographical information on him at **www. unithistories.com/officers/RAFVR_officers_B01.html**.

(iii) Royal Navy

Prior to the union with England in 1707, there was a separate Royal Scots Navy, though after James VI became James I of England in 1603 it became less important to the defence of Scotland. A useful text on the subject is J. Grant's *The Old Scots Navy 1689-1710* (Navy Records Society 1904), which has been transcribed and made available via the Electric Scotland website at **www.electricscotland.com/history/navy/index.htm**. As with the army, the availability of modern Royal Naval records from 1707 will depend on the rank of your ancestor and the period in which he served. A useful TNA guide to the various records for the service is found online at **www.nationalarchives.gov.uk/ family history/military/navy**.

The main source for naval officers' service records from 1756 is found at TNA's Admiralty records section, ADM 196, with many digitised and made available through the Documents Online service. For officers commissioned after 1917, TNA does not hold records, and you will need to apply to the Ministry of Defence through **www.veterans-uk.info/service_records/service_records.html**.

For junior ratings who served prior to 1853 there are no service records, only ships muster and pay lists, held under the accession numbers ADM 36-39, ADM 115 and ADM 177, but you will need to know which ship your man served on. Pension records from 1801 to 1844 are indexed by crewmen's names at TNA under ADM 29. Personnel records for ratings from 1853-79 are held under ADM 139, whilst those from 1873-1927 have been digitised from ADM 188 and made available through the Documents Online service for a fee, which include a summary of service up to 1927.

The Documents Online service has various other digitised records for the Royal Marines, the Royal Naval Division (seamen who fought with the army in WW1), officers' service records, the Women's Royal Naval Service, a collection of 20,000 wills from seamen between 1786 and 1882, and more. If your ancestor fought at Trafalgar, TNA also has an interesting online site at **www.nationalarchives.gov.uk/trafalgarancestors** listing those who took part in Nelson's fleet.

FamilyRelatives.com has a British Naval Biographical Dictionary from 1849 amongst its holdings, with information on ranks from Lieutenant up to Admiral of the Fleet. Also on the site is the Commissioned Sea Officers of the Royal Navy 1660-1815 database compiled by an Admiralty librarian called David Bonner Smith from various sources, again, purely for officers.

The Forty Five

The most famous rebellion in Scotland was that of the 'Forty Five', the 1745-46 campaign of Prince Charles Edward Stuart to reclaim the British throne which had been taken from his grandfather James VII (II of Britain) in 1689. The definitive account of the battle which sealed Bonnie Prince Charlie's fate is John Prebble's book *Culloden*, first published in 1961.

There are many sources that can help to trace family members who may have fought with the Jacobites. A ten volume series of books entitled *The Lyon in Mourning*, a gathering of letters, journals and eye witness accounts, was gathered in the immediate aftermath of the campaign by the Episcopalian minister Reverend Robert Forbes. These were later edited by Henry Paton in 1896 for the Scottish History Society, and republished in 1975 by the Scottish Academic Press. The accounts have since been digitised by the National Library of Scotland and made available at **www.nls.uk/print/transcriptions/index. html**. A three volume series of books entitled *The Memoirs of the Jacobites of 1715 and 1745*, produced in 1845 by Mrs Thomson, has also been transcribed by the project Guttenberg team and made available at **www.electricscotland. com/history/books.htm**.

S. & N. Genealogy Supplies Ltd (**www.GenealogySupplies.com**) has released a CD entitled *A List of Persons Concerned in the Rebellion 1745-46*, containing a digitised facsimile of a book first produced by the SHS in 1890. This account was in turn based on a list of Jacobite rebels compiled in September 1747 by the Queen's Remembrancer, which named many of those who had fought at Culloden.

Bruce Gordon Seton's *The Prisoners of the '45*, also published by the SHS in 1928, is a collation of the names of arrested Jacobites, with a description of their fate and a note of the sources used to identify them. More recently *No Quarter Given: The Muster Roll of Prince Charles Edward Stuart's Army, 1745-46* has been produced by Christine Aikman, Alastair Livingstone and Betty Stuart-Hart (Neil Wilson Publishing, 3rd ed. 2001), based on muster rolls drawn up by the Government following the battle. Many landowners who took the wrong side in the conflict had their estates forfeited (as did many from the earlier rising of 1715) – records concerning the management of their lands following forfeiture are found at NAS under E600-687, and E701-788.

On the Hanoverian side, a full regimental list is available at **http://en. wikipedia.org/wiki/Battle_of_Culloden** with links to websites showing where to obtain more information. Military records are scant for this period, but if your ancestor was an officer he will be easier to trace. The surviving records will be listed in Roper's *The Records of the War Office and Related Departments 1660-1994* (PRO, 1994).

Merchant Navy

Records for ancestors who worked in the Merchant Navy can be located in many locations across England and Scotland. The most comprehensive guide to their location is *My Ancestor was a Merchant Seaman* by Christopher and Michael Watts (see Further Reading).

Amongst the Scottish collections in which to search for your earliest mariners are various port entry books held in the NAS under E 71 (up to 1640), E 72 (1661-1696) and E 504 (1742-1830), listing the names of ships' masters only, and crew bounty payment books for those who engaged in herring fishing and whaling between 1750 and 1825, held under E 502 and E 508.

A rich source for merchant shipping is the records of the Customs and Excise office, and a useful guide to what is held at NAS is found at **www.nas.gov.uk/guides/customs.asp**. Registers of Shipping, maintained by customs officials from 1786 onwards, list the owners of vessels engaged in the merchant trades, and are held at both NAS and in local archives. In the west of Scotland, records for fishing vessels were kept with the Fishery Board records from 1869-1988 and are held under AF 17-AF 62 at the NAS. Justice for all maritime cases up to 1830, both civil and criminal, was administered by the High Court of Admiralty, with records listed at the NAS under AC 9, AC 10, AC 15 and AC 16.

At the ScotlandsPeople Centre, a list of 1851 seamen's crew lists, drawn from records held at the National Archives at Kew under BT 98, is available to view on the e-library. The records cover Aberdeenshire, Angus, Lanarkshire, Renfrewshire, Scotland South-East, Scotland South-West and the Highlands and Islands, and list age, place of birth, rank and ticket number, whilst there is also a Master index for Scotland, Ireland and Wales.

There are some online collections which can assist your research. Eddie Connolly's Northern Irish records extracts website Eddie's Extracts (**http://freepages.genealogy.rootsweb.ancestry.com/~econnolly/**) contains an index to the *Register of Deceased Seamen* for Shetland from 1911-1925 , and for Orkney from 1911-1924, which gives a wealth of information, including last known abode, name of ship, birth place, date of death, cause, and more.

For more recent ancestors, merchant seamen arrested in German ports upon the outbreak of World War 1 are listed in Marcus Bateman's *British Seamen and Civilian Prisoners of War* page at **http://wanborough.ukuhost.co.uk/POW/POW.htm**, derived from records held at TNA under MT 9/1238, whilst many biographical entries for those who were interned at Ruhleben, near Berlin, can be found at *The Ruhleben Story*, located at **http://ruhleben.tripod.com**. Records of medals issued to merchant seamen during World War Two are available at TNA's Documents Online service, listing all medals claimed from 1946 to 2002, whilst a series of World War Two Merchant Shipping Movement cards are also there, though these can only be searched by the name of the ship (or its former name).

Ancestry (**www.ancestry.co.uk**) also hosts a copy of David Dobson's extremely useful research guide *Scottish Maritime Records 1600-1850* (first published in 1999), covering everything from the merchant navy and whaling to smuggling and privateering. The author has also produced a series of books under the banner of 'Mariners of ...', with titles including *Mariners of Kirlkcaldy, St. Andrews and Fife 1600-1800, Mariners of Aberdeen and Northern Scotland 1600-1800, Mariners of the Lothians 1600-1800*, and more. For more information, visit David's site at **www.btinternet.com/~lds.dobson.**

Church ministers

Biographical entries on all ministers to have worked within the established Church of Scotland are available in a series of volumes known as *Fasti Ecclesiae Scoticanae*, first published in 1866 and revised again in the early Twentieth Century. These are available at many libraries and at the ScotlandsPeople Centre in Edinburgh, but can also be found online at two websites. The first at **www.archive.org/ search.php?query=Fasti% 20AND%20mediatype%3Atexts&page=2** has all volumes of the revised edition, which can be viewed on the site or downloaded in text or PDF formats (Volume 5, covering the Synods of Fife, Angus and Mearns, is unfortunately very badly digitised and difficult to read). The second site at **www.dwalker.pwp.blueyonder.co.uk/Ministers% 20Index.htm** contains transcriptions of the first two revised volumes in the series, published in 1915. These cover i) the Synods of Lothian and Tweeddale, and ii) the Synods of Merse and Teviotdale Dumfries and Galloway. Copies of later volumes can also be purchased on CD from this site.

For other denominations there are similar volumes, including the two volume *History of the Congregations of the United Presbyterian Church 1733-1900*, written by the Reverend Robert Small and published in 1904 (available online at **www.archive.org/ stream/historyofpresbyt01smaluoft/historyofpresbyt01smaluoft_djvu.txt**), the *Fasti of the United Free Church of Scotland 1920-1929* by the Reverend John Alexander Laws, published by Oliver & Boyd in Edinburgh in 1956, and *Scottish Episcopal Clergy 1689-2000* by David M. Bertie, published by T. and T. Clark in 2000 (a limited preview is available on Google Books) .

A free to access database also of use is the *Surman Index*, which lists 32,000 Congregational and Presbyterian ministers who have practised in England and Wales between the mid 17th century and 1972. The index has been digitised and made available at **http://surman.english.qmul.ac.uk**. Compiled by Charles Surman and held at the Dr. Williams Centre for Dissenting Studies in London, the card index and database includes a great deal of information on dissenting ministers who trained and practised in Scotland. A list of obituaries from 1900 – 2004 for the Unitarian Church at **www.unitarian societies.org.uk/historical/ministerobit.html** also includes many Scots who served the Church in a ministerial capacity.

Burgh trades

Prior to the 15th century, tradesmen working in the country's burghs had to be members of the Merchant Guild. On March 12th 1424 an Act of Parliament was passed declaring that *"in each town of the realm there be chosen, of each sundry craft used therein, a wise man of that craft by the rest of that craft and the counsel of the officers of the town, who shall be held deacon or master over the rest for the time assigned to him, to assay and govern all works that are made by the workmen of his craft, so that the king's lieges are not defrauded in the future as they have been in the past by untrue men of crafts".* This paved the way for the creation of trade corporations and guilds in Scotland, designed to protect the rights of masons, weavers, hammermen, glovers, skinners, bakers, and other skilled crafts, which required their members to first serve apprenticeships.

Records for these guilds and corporations, if they have survived, can provide a wealth of information on your earlier ancestors. Most are held at county record archives, though some remain in private hands, and they can be sourced using the SCAN and NRAS catalogues (see Chapter 2).

To be able to vote in an election within the guilds, and to be able to practise a trade within the burgh, you had to have a burgess ticket or the freedom of your 'calling'. You could gain this by marrying a burgess's or freeman's daughter, by serving an apprenticeship with a freeman, by hereditary right if your father was already a freeman or burgess, or by purchase (often at extortionate prices), particularly if you were an outsider. In some instances a person may have even been granted an honorary burgess ticket or freedom for some notable deed of benefit to the trade.

For apprenticeships, many guilds kept their own indenture books, recording the conditions, duration and financial terms of an agreement between a prospective apprentice and his master. Following the completion of the indenture the apprentice became a journeyman, and records will also show bookings of these to various masters in the parish or beyond. From 1710-1804, a stamp duty was imposed on masters taking on apprentices, and a record of these payments can be found within the *Apprenticeship Books* in the National Archives at Kew, located under IR 1. Entries go as far as 1811 in

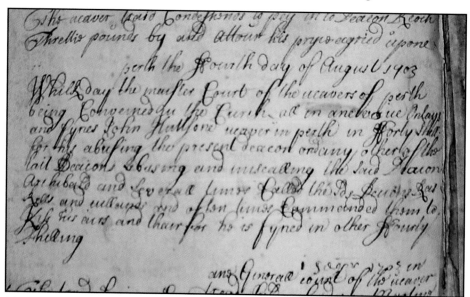

John Hutson's case from 1703, as recorded within the minutes of the Weavers Incorporation of Perth.

the books, as payments could be made as late as the year after an apprentice completed his indenture period. A copy of the entries from 1710-1774 is held at the Society of Genealogists in London, and is also available online at the Origins Network (**www.originsnetwork.com/help/popup-aboutbo-appgb2.htm**) – of the 350,000 entries featured, about a fifth are Scottish.

Other records kept by the guilds and incorporations include minute books, which often recorded the adjudications of courts set up to deal with the indiscretions of their members. One of my favourite all time entries in such books was recorded within the minute books of the Weavers Incorporation of Perth. On August 4th 1703, a certain John Hutson was tried by the trade's Deacon's court and was subsequently fined forty shillings *"for his abusing the present Deacon and any other of the laite Deacons"* and for having *"called the s[ai]d Deacons Raskells and villainds"*. As if this crime was not heinous enough, Hutson also *"often times commanded them to kiss his airs"* for which he was fined an additional forty shillings!

A list of trades records held at the NAS is available at **www.nas.gov.uk/guides/crafts.asp**. Databases for burgess records and apprenticeships for Edinburgh can also be found online at **www.scotsfind.org/databases_free/freedatabaseindex.htm**. A useful article in the eleventh edition of the *Family and Local History Handbook* (**www.genealogical.co.uk**) is *'Trafficking Burgesses: Exploring records of the Scottish Royal Burghs'* by Rosemary Bigwood.

> ### Tip: SCAN Knowledge Base
> The Scottish Archives Network's Knowledge Base page at *www.scan.org.uk/knowledgebase/index.htm* has many useful sections on Scottish industries, including lighthouses, policing, banking, and more.

Crofters

Crofters are farmers with small agricultural holdings in the Highlands and Islands. During the 19th century they were badly affected by the Clearances, and fought a long campaign to gain land rights in the late 19th and early 20th centuries.

If your ancestor was a crofter, a useful resource is the crofting section of the Am Baile website at **www.ambaile.org** which includes the *Crofter* newspaper from the 1880s, whilst the four volume Napier Commission of 1884, which investigated the grievances of the crofting community across the north of Scotland, can be read online at the Lochaber College website at both **www.highland-elibrary.com/7.html** and **http://lochaber.uhi.ac.uk/links/napier-commission**.

Miners

If your ancestor was a miner, there are three main websites that can be of assistance. The first is the Scottish Mining Website at **www.scottishmining.co.uk**, which amongst its many impressive holdings holds a mining accident section, notes on miners' houses (a series commissioned by the Glasgow Herald in 1875), and a breakdown of individual mining parishes with unique records for each area. For Scottish women working in the pits, a list of deaths from 1851-1914 can be found at **http://freepages.genealogy. rootsweb.ancestry.com/~stenhouse/coal/pbl/Scotland/disct.htm**.

The Coalmining History Resource Centre website at **www.cmhrc.co.uk** also has a fully searchable database of British accidents in mines, as well as maps showing the locations of mines and more.

The NAS is also worth visiting if you had an ancestor involved in an accident between 1861 and 1895, as there may be further information in the Procedure Books of the Lord Advocate's records series under AD12/19-21, whilst from 1895 onwards there may be a fatal accident enquiry recorded within the sheriff court records held at the centre.

Police

There are several police archives around the country, such as the Glasgow Police Heritage Society Archives based in Glasgow's Merchant City (**www.policemuseum.org.uk**), which holds records of Britain's first ever police force from 1779 to 1975.

Many county archives hold local records also, such as the Glasgow Archives (at the Mitchell Library), which has various police force registers from the west of Scotland, including Glasgow, Dunbartonshire, Lanarkshire and Renfrewshire. Most police forces in Scotland have information concerning their respective archives, and many useful records can also be sourced from the SCAN catalogue (Chapter 2).

Google Books (**http://books.google.com**) has various manuals and digests of the law of Scotland from 1824, 1847, 1855, 1865 and 1880, which not only illustrate the changing nature of Scottish law throughout the 19th century, but also the roles and responsibilities of the various Scottish Police forces across the country.

Doctors and Nurses

Scotland has for centuries been internationally renowned for the quality and skills of its medical practitioners. The Royal College of Surgeons of Edinburgh was established in 1505 and its records can be consulted in the college's library, which has an online catalogue at **www.rcsed.ac.uk/site/355/default.aspx**.

If your ancestor was a physician, it is worth investigating whether he joined the Royal College of Physicians of Edinburgh, the website for which, at **www.rcpe.ac.uk/ library/index.php**, provides information on its archive holdings.

Modern day general practitioners emerged as a profession in the early 19th century. Two essential resources worth consulting for these are the annually produced *Medical Directory* (first established in 1845), and the more detailed *Medical Register* (from 1859). These provide information on the qualifications and careers of those practising medicine, and are available in most major public libraries, as well as on Ancestry (**www.ancestry.co.uk**), whilst many are also available free of charge at Google Books (**http://books.google.com**). A comprehensive history of the National Health Service in Scotland, established in 1948, is located at **www.60yearsofnhsscotland.co.uk**.

On the nursing front, a useful research resource is the website of the British Red Cross at **www.redcross.org.uk/standard.asp?id=2623**. Established in 1870, the Red

Cross was instrumental during the First World War and many subsequent conflicts.

The NAS also holds some nursing records, including various registers of trained nurses appointed by the Scottish Board of Health to poorhouses between 1885 and 1930 at HH2/33 to HH2/36, and registers of nursing examination candidates, appointments and exams passed at HH2-37. Further south, TNA at Kew is particularly useful for the records of nurses in wartime service, and its Military Records Information Sheet No. 55 is located online at **www.nationalarchives.gov.uk/catalogue/RdLeaflet.asp?s LeafletID=169**. As all nurses had to be registered by the State in 1925, TNA is equally useful for finding the records of those registered, which are catalogued under DT 10-14, with the nurses' examinations recorded under DT 22-32.

With regard to ambulance work, St Andrew's Ambulance Association was established in Glasgow in 1882. The society's records are in private hands, and can be found through the NRAS catalogue (Chapter 2) under accession number NRAS 1394. Further information on St Andrew's Ambulance can also be found at **www.firstaid.org.uk**.

Further Reading

FOWLER, Simon (2006) *Tracing Your Army Ancestors*. Barnsley: Pen and Sword Books Ltd.

GIBSON, Jeremy, and MEDLYCOTT, Mervyn (1994) *Militia Lists and Musters 1757-1876 (4th edition)*. Bury: Federation of Family History Societies, 1994.

GLENDINNING, Miles, and MARTINS, Susanna Wade (2009) *Buildings of the Land: Scotland's Farms 1750-2000*. Edinburgh: Royal Commission on the Ancient and Historical Monuments of Scotland

MULHERN, BEECH & THOMPSON, eds. (2008) *Scottish Life and Society Volume 7: The Working Life of the Scots*. Edinburgh: John Donald (Birlinn).

SMOUT, T. C. (1969) *A History of the Scottish People 1560-1830*. London: William Collins and Sons.

SMOUT, T. C. (1987) *A Century of the Scottish People 1830-1950*. London: William Collins and Sons.

WATTS, Christopher T. and Michael J. (2002) *My Ancestor Was a Merchant Seaman*. London: Society of Genealogists Enterprises Ltd.

10. *DNA*

The use of DNA analysis in genealogy is becoming increasingly more common, and whilst it may have limited applications for your research, it may also be able to provide a breakthrough when all other sources have yielded no solutions.

Paternal line ancestry

There are various types of DNA which can be analysed, but the most useful test genealogically is one for Y-chromosome DNA. This form of DNA can only be inherited by a son from his father, and as a son also inherits his surname from his father in Scotland, theoretically both should be passed down the centuries together on the male line. This means that several generations down the line from a common ancestor, distant male cousins should not only have the same surname, but also very closely matching genetic profiles. Whilst only men can take such a test, known as a 'Y-DNA test', women can still ask their fathers, brothers, uncles or some other male relative to take one on their behalf in order to follow their paternal ancestry.

DNA results can both confirm a known relationship and proactively help you to look for possible cousins further afield, particularly when no paper trail exists. The discovery of a match between your profile and that of a distant relative on a DNA database may allow you to contact that person and perhaps discover documents that can help you to either break through the brick wall on your own line or to work your way around it. Imagine, for example, if this new found cousin turns out to have the family bible from 200 years ago with the names of your ancestors included, information that goes well before the point at which you are stuck!

Something along this line happened to a friend of mine, Alasdair MacDonald, who took a Y-DNA test through a company called FamilyTree DNA (**www.familytree dna.com**), and duly submitted the results to a MacDonald surname database. His earliest confirmed ancestor through the paper trail had been established as a Donald MacDonald, born circa 1750 in Halkirk parish, Caithness – not the natural haunting grounds of the MacDonalds! After submitting his DNA results, Alasdair was soon contacted by a gentleman from the Republic of Suriname in South America, who had an almost identical genetic profile, and the results suggested that that they shared a very late 17th century ancestor, just beyond his present brick wall. One of the gent's ancestors had settled in South America in the 1820s to work as an overseer on a plantation, but he had traced the line further back to a John MacDonald, an 18th century cattle drover from the same Caithness parish of Halkirk, who it is believed was a possible brother or cousin to Donald. As John's life was much better documented within the area, Alasdair now has a new source that can help him understand the nature of his family's presence in the area at that time.

The real surprise for Alasdair, however, was to discover that his DNA profile had much more in common with the MacNeil clan from the Island of Barra than that of the MacDonalds. This suggests that somewhere along the line there may have been a so-called 'non-paternity event', where a MacNeil at some point fathered a male child who took on the surname of MacDonald, perhaps because it was the surname of the boy's mother, or because he was adopted by someone of that name. This aspect of DNA research can be particularly useful to Scottish genealogy, with its long established heritage of Highland clans. The idea that a particular clan is comprised of lots of people all related to a common ancestor, and who all have the same surname, is a myth. The clans were more of a social and political grouping centered round a particular family in an area, providing a feudal obligation to a chief in return for protection from its enemies. Not everybody living in such territories necessarily shared the same ancestry, and may well have taken on the clan surname simply to show fealty to the chief. DNA can therefore be used to help identify the individual origins of those who came together to form the main clan unit.

Websites carrying DNA profiles for Scottish clans include a project for Clan Donald located at **http://dna-project.clan-donald-usa.org**, which tries to group people into the various family groups that descended in the Western Isles from Somerled, the 12th century warrior who was the progenitor of the MacDonald clan, and other related lines

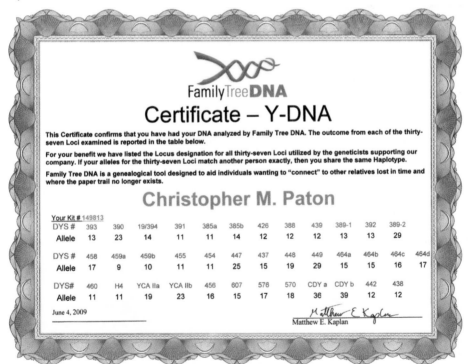

My Y-DNA profile results, from a FamilyTree DNA 37 marker test.

such as the MacAllisters and MacDougalls. Other projects include that for Clan Fraser at **www.familytreedna.com/public/Clan_Fraser**, whilst more generically additional clan projects can be located at **www.ourfamilyorigins.com/scotland/dna.htm** and **www.scottishdna.net/s-dna.html**. As well as surname based databases there are also various sites set up along territorial lines, such as the *Isles of the Hebrides* project at **www.familytreedna.com/public/isleofislay**, and another on Shetland located at **www.davidkfaux.org/shetlandislandsY-DNA**, which seeks to identify the origins of the local populations and to plot their migrations within and beyond the islands.

Even if your ancestor was not a part of a clan – and remember the clan system was only based within the Highlands and Islands – there are many other surname projects to which you can submit your result. The Y-Search database at **www.ysearch.org** is perhaps the best known, set up by the market leading testing company Family Tree DNA (**www.familytreedna.com**), which as with the above mentioned sites will also accept results from many other testing companies. Y-base (**www.y-base.org**) is another, operating along similar lines. WorldFamilies.net (**www.worldfamilies.net**) is an educational resource offering some useful lists for surname based projects, and members of the Guild of One Name Studies have also initiated many DNA surname projects (see Chapter 2).

Illegitimacy and adoption

A further scenario where DNA testing might prove to be useful is with regard to illegitimacy. If I know that one of my direct line male ancestors was stated to have been illegitimate, a Y-DNA test might be able to help me identify the natural father. If I have an idea about who the suspected father was, I can then try and trace a known male descendant from him, and then ask that person to take a Y-DNA test. If he agrees and his profile matches mine, then this will strongly suggest that his ancestor was indeed my illegitimate ancestor's father, though the possibility still exists that it may have been a sibling or cousin of his with the same surname.

Such a test can also be handy for those who have been adopted when trying to gain an idea about the possible identity of their natural father. A test may show that the father has a DNA profile which resembles that of somebody by the name of Robertson. It won't confirm that the father is definitely a Robertson, but it is a very useful starting point if no other clues are forthcoming.

The test

When taking a Y-DNA test, various points on the DNA of your Y-chromosome are examined, known as 'markers'. At each point a numerical value is noted, known as an 'allele'. Your DNA profile is therefore basically a list of these marker points that have been examined, and the value recorded beside each of them. The markers tend to have complicated names such as YGAAT1B07 or DYS459b (and the names for the same marker may vary depending on the testing company!), but don't let that put you off. Just think of each as 'point 1' on your DNA chain, 'point 2' on the chain, etc. The following is an example of three of the thirty seven markers examined from my Y-chromosome by Family Tree DNA:

Marker	Value
DYS393	13
DYS385a	11
DYS385b	14
Etc...	

Most DNA test providers will offer a basic package that looks at 37 such markers, but you can examine additional markers for a further fee. The more you examine, the more accurate will be your result, but the test will also be more expensive. To provide a sample, most labs will ask you to rub a series of swabs on the inside of your cheek for about 60 seconds, and then place them into a protective cover such as a small plastic phial, which you then post off to the laboratory. The results usually take about a month to process.

Once you have them, the next step is to then look for matches in the aforementioned databases. Without comparing your results to somebody else's on a surname or clan based project, your results will be next to useless.

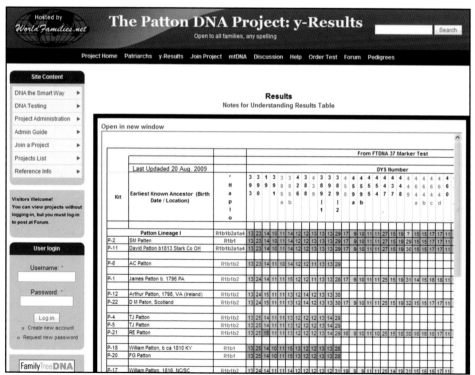

An online Y-DNA surname project can allow you to search for genetic matches for your profile.

Haplogroups

In addition to your marker values on the Y-DNA test, make sure you take a note of your 'haplogroup' value also. This identifies which branch of the tree of mankind you belong to, which can help to show how your ancestors made their way across Europe to Scotland. Both Y-DNA tests and mtDNA tests will provide you with a haplogroup for your paternal and maternal lines – my paternal haplogroup, for example, is noted as 'R', which I share with millions of other people in Britain and Ireland. Most DNA service providers have websites showing how these migrations occurred, to try and explain what is known as your 'deep ancestry'. Genealogically it really is of no use to your research, though it may be fun to know where your umpteenth great grandfather Ug the Caveman was out hunting for woolly mammoths! However, it is theoretically possible that somebody on a DNA database can have exact matching values as myself on the same 37 markers, but in fact be completely unrelated, as he may be from a completely different haplogroup, though this happens rarely.

Maternal line ancestry

Another test that can be taken is that for mitochondrial DNA, or mtDNA, which is only passed on by a mother to her children. Your mother will have inherited her mtDNA from your maternal grandmother, who in turn inherited it from her mother, and so on. Whilst men cannot pass on this type of DNA to their children, they still have it, and can still be tested for it. Whether a man or a woman is tested, the information that is obtained will refer only to maternal line ancestors, in much the same way as a Y-DNA test works only for paternal line ancestors.

The problem here is that the names of Scottish women on a maternal line going back constantly change from generation to generation, so you cannot compare your results with other people in a surname project in the same way that you would with a Y-DNA profile. You can still upload your results to a project on mitochondrial DNA database, such as that at Mitosearch (**www.mitosearch.org**), either for a geographical area or for a particular haplogroup, to try and find matches. This rarely produces a useful result however, the problem being that mitochondrial DNA mutates very slowly, and so most times that a database flags up a possible match, it will tend to be so vague a connection that it will be next to useless.

The mtDNA profile can actually be taken from the same sample that you gave for your Y-DNA test, but the results are presented in a very different way. The following is my complete mtDNA profile:

HVR1	16519	C	(T)
HVR2	263	G	(A)
HVR3	315.1	C	(-)

(Haplogroup – H)

I hope you didn't blink there, as you might have missed it! With a Y-DNA test, you get a long list of marker points and values, but with a mitochondrial DNA test, you get a result based on a comparison to the results of a woman whose mtDNA was tested in 1981 in Cambridge, and whose profile therefore became known as the 'Cambridge Reference Sequence'. Rather than detail what my entire profile is, the mtDNA result tells me at which points my profile differs to hers. The bottom line with mitochondrial DNA tests is that they are much less useful genealogically than Y-DNA tests.

Tips: DNA service providers

*There are various DNA test providers in addition to the aforementioned FamilyTree DNA and DNA Ancestry services, providing both Y-DNA and mtDNA tests. Genetree (**www.genetree.com**) is a service working in collaboration with the Sorenson Molecular Genealogy Foundation in Utah, whilst 23andme (**www.23andme.com**) is a New York based company that also offers a comparable service. DNA Heritage is another useful service at **www.dnaheritage.com**. A useful website to help compare the different suppliers, and what they offer, is that of the International Society of Genetic Genealogy at **www.isogg.org**.*

Futher Reading

POMEROY, Chris (2007) *Family History in the Genes*. London: The National Archives.

SMOLENYAK, Megan Smolenyak, and TURNER, Ann (2005) *Trace your Roots with DNA*. Rodale Press.

SYKES, Brian (2001) *The Seven Daughters of Eve*. London: Bantam Press.

11. *Heraldry and Tartans*

The Court of the Lord Lyon, based at HM New Register House in Edinburgh, is responsible for all matters in Scotland relating to heraldry. In addition to granting new coats of arms, its highest official, the Lord Lyon King of Arms, also has the power to fine anybody illegally using a coat of arms that is not his or hers to display, a right which he has enjoyed since 1592. He is also responsible for all ceremonial matters of state within the country. In addition to the Lord Lyon there are Her Majesty's Officers of Arms, which at the time of writing consisted of three Heralds (Albany Herald, Rothesay Herald and Ross Herald) and three Pursuivants (Carrick Pursuivant, Unicorn Pursuivant, and Ormond Pursuivant).

In Scotland, Arms can be granted to a person only if they are deemed by the Lord Lyon to be 'virtuous and well deserving', and come within his jurisdiction. Anybody born or resident within Scotland, and within parts of the British Commonwealth, can apply for a *Grant of Arms*. For those living in England, Wales or Ireland, applications for these grants must be made to their own respective heraldic authorities.

There is an initial lodging fee of £200, which will be offset against the final dues. If you are applying for a new coat of arms, the minimum cost for a shield with or without a motto is, at the time of

The Arms of the Lord Lyon King of Arms.

writing, £1194, whilst at the higher end of the scale, a grant for a shield, crest, motto and supporters for a commercial organisation will cost £3596, though it should be noted that it is rare for supporters to be granted.

If, however, you have an ancestor with the same surname who was 'armigerous', i.e. had a coat of arms recorded in the Public Register of All Arms and Bearings (see below), you can apply to have a version of those Arms recorded for yourself. These are known as 'matriculated' Arms, and the cost of the 'recording' varies depending on what is required.

Use of arms

If a member of the family has a coat of arms, it is not permitted for everyone in the family to use the same Arms, and a matriculation must therefore be approved for use by the Lord Lyon. This 'differencing' of Arms is actually quite scientific in how it is carried out. An eldest son will bear an achievement with a unique temporary standard difference to his father's design included, whilst his brother's Arms will carry another separate variation, and so on. When their father eventually passes away the eldest son will inherit his Arms, as these are treated as heritable property. It is extremely important to note that, despite the general belief or the tourist hype, there is no such thing as a 'family coat of arms'. However, the crest of a clan chief can be adopted and worn as a badge by the family and members of the extended clan wishing to show loyalty to him or her.

The design

The shields and crests have a long and wonderful design tradition going back to the 12th century, comprising various elements of which the most important is the *shield* itself. The basic colours used are the metals of gold and silver (known as 'or' and 'argent'), and the five main colours of red ('gules'), blue ('azure'), green ('vert'), black ('sable') and purple ('purpure'). A fundamental rule in heraldry is that a metallic colour cannot be set against another metal, or a colour against a colour.

In addition to the shield in a full coat of arms (or *'heraldic achievement'*) you will then find *supporters* on either side, usually in the form of two animals or mythical creatures, and above it a *helm* and/or *crown* or *coronet*, on top of which you will find a crest (used as the clan *badge*). This is separated from the helm by a *wreath*, essentially a twisted bit of cloth, and cloth *mantling*, which drapes behind the helm, usually in a very stylised manner. Above this is then located the *motto* or *slughorn* (from Gaelic *'sluagh gairm'*, meaning *'war cry'*), whilst the shield and supporters have a *compartment* to the base on which they stand.

An achievement can also be expressed in a written form known as a *blazon*, which describes all aspects of the design. As an example, the following is the blazon used to describe the shield of the Lord Lyon King of Arms:

> *Argent, a lion sejant affrontée Gules holding in his dexter paw a thistle slipped Vert, flowered Proper, and in the sinister a shield Gules, on a chief Azure a saltire of the First.*

So scientific is the manner in which achievements are constructed that once the basic rules and methodology are understood it is possible to decode it to understand a person's ancestry, sometimes for several generations going back.

Locating coats of arms

The official record of all Scottish coats of arms is the Public Register of All Arms and Bearings in Scotland. First established in 1672, the register contains written blazons and in some cases a brief genealogy, and, from Volume 2 (from 1804), the blazons are accompanied by hand painted depictions of the Arms granted, and a brief summary of the genealogies of the petitioners if recorded when the application was made. This may go back a mere generation or two, or considerably further if an ancestor was also armigerous. The register has been digitised and made available to view at the ScotlandsPeople Centre, with the digitised coverage up to one hundred years ago (with the records available therefore updated each year). The records can also be downloaded from the external website at **www.scotlandspeople.gov.uk** for a £10 fee, though the index is free to search.

In addition to the public register, blazons for many coats of arms predating 1672 can be consulted online for free through the website of the Heraldry Society of Scotland at **www.heraldry-scotland.co.uk/mitchell.html**. This details many Scottish rolls and armorials held in institutions such as the Court of the Lord Lyon, National Library of Scotland and the British Museum in London, as well as within private hands and foreign archives. The earliest listed is the *Balliol Roll* from 1332.

Tip: Blue Blood
Many members of the peerage and titled classes of Scotland have had their arms and pedigrees recorded in armorials, such as Burke's Peerage (www.burkes-peerage.net) and Debrett's Peerage (www.debretts.com/debrett's-publications/ books/peerage-and-baronetage-2008.aspx). Specialist websites listing the histories of many titled families include Stirnet (www.stirnet.com) and ThePeerage.com (www.thepeerage.com). As with any published pedigree, when doing your research, make sure to verify all claims before adopting the families into your own tree.

Tartan

There is a lot of hype and nonsense surrounding tartans and kilts, and about who is entitled to wear what and when. Despite the modern spin put out by the tartan industry, ancient tartans before the days of Bonnie Prince Charlie were not individually linked to particular clans and septs, but based on what organic materials could be found locally to make simple dyes for the patterns, meaning that many clans wore tartans of similar designs and colours. Jacobites on the battlefield of Culloden wore a white cockade to distinguish friend from foe, they did not go about examining each other's kilts!

It was not until a visit by George IV to Edinburgh in 1822 that the modern day tradition of a clan tartan was really invented, when the efforts of Sir Walter Scott and others to romanticise Highland culture made it a trendy piece of garb to wear. This was further compounded with the fascination shown by Queen Victoria to the garment when she moved to Scotland a few decades later. Cashing in on the interest in the designs, two brothers claiming descent from the Sobieski Stuarts (and therefore from Bonnie Prince Charlie), produced a document called the 'Vestiarium Scoticum', listing many alleged ancient tartan designs that they claimed to have found in an old manuscript, which they somehow never got around to showing anybody! Now everybody and their granny wanted to wear a piece of tartan, and specifically a design to represent 'their' clan, whether they were Highlanders or Lowlanders, despite the fact that a lot of it was simply fraudulent in its provenance. Several interesting articles on the history of tartan can be read at the Scottish Tartans Authority website at **www.tartansauthority.com**.

Whilst it is important to note that a lot of the so called ancient tartans have very doubtful origins, it is also equally important to note that tartan is still nevertheless a very well entrenched Scottish tradition – it is just a very modern one. As such, old photographs of family members in Highland dress may still turn out to be useful for your research. If you have an image of somebody in a particular tartan, it may provide a clue to their identity, as it may very well be that the reason the subject is wearing a MacLeod tartan is because he or she is indeed a MacLeod, and wearing the same design that all MacLeods wear as defined by the modern tartan industry. Whether that means they can claim a descent from the ancient chiefs of old is quite another matter!

The Scottish Register of Tartans was formally established on February 5th 2009, and is administered by the National Archives of Scotland, headed by the Keeper of the Records of Scotland. With an online presence at **www.tartanregister.gov.uk**, the register incorporates designs from earlier databases such as the Scottish Tartans Authority and the Scottish World Tartans Register (**www.scottish-tartans-world-register.com**), as well as newly registered designs with the authority, providing a source for literally thousands of tartans. The website not only provides an online encyclopaedia for these patterns, but also allows users to register new designs, to request technical information such as thread counts, and more.

The Clans

In Highland Scotland, and in the Western Isles, Gaelic (Gàidhlig) was the main spoken language for centuries, and family life was centred around the clan, derived from the Gaelic word 'clann', meaning 'children'. The chief presided over the population of a local territory from a strong defendable vantage point, and could call upon his men to provide military service in times of war. Not everybody in the clan was related by blood, and many different families would show fealty to the chief by taking on the clan name. It is therefore dangerous to assume that just because your ancestor carried the name MacLeod that he was necessary a descendant of the Norse warrior Leod.

Many clan names begin with 'Mac', the Gaelic word for 'son of', but when written in Gaelic itself some of these clan names drop the prefix. A good example is MacDonald, which in Gaelic is 'Domhnallach'. When this happens, it is a fair bet that the family does not come from a Gaelic origin. Many perceived clans were not in fact clans at all, but families of Norse or other origins which came to live in the Gaelic lifestyle, such as the Grahams (na Greumach) and the Chisholms (na Siosolaich).

A list of clans with links to their own dedicated websites can be found at www.rampantscotland.com/clans.

Meeting the present Duke of Montrose, chief of the Grahams, at the Gathering in Edinburgh, July 2009.

Further Reading

ANON (1999) *Scottish Heraldry* [booklet]. Edinburgh: The Heraldry Society of Scotland

FOX-DAVIES, Arthur (1978) *A Complete Guide to Heraldry*. New York: Bonanza Books.

INNES, Sir Thomas, of Learney (1956) *Scots Heraldry*. Edinburgh: Oliver & Boyd.

NEWTON, Michael (2009) *Warriors of the Word: The World of the Scottish Highlanders*. Edinburgh: Birlinn Ltd.

12. *Other Sources*

Newspapers

Newspapers can be a wonderful resource for bringing the personalities and stories of your ancestors to life. Towards the end of the 19th century people increasingly began to place notices regarding births, marriages and deaths for family members in papers, as well as burial notices and memorial entries. Sometimes a family may have been too traumatised to place a death notice in the paper, but may have been inclined soon after to place a message of thanks directed to those who had helped the family with the funeral arrangements etc, so it is always worth checking a couple of weeks after the event just in case. Occasionally you may also find notices of relatives or ancestors who died overseas, which can be especially useful.

As well as intimations columns, you may be fortunate enough to find your ancestor actually making the news – or unfortunately, as the case may be! A good example lies with the death of a Peter Stewart, who died in a coal mining accident in Kilwinning, as recorded in the Ardrossan & Saltcoats Herald of June 4th 1864:

FATAL ACCIDENT
On Thursday morning, last week, a miner, named Peter Stewart, was killed in Millburn pit, Fergushill Colliery, by a portion of the roof falling upon him while engaged at his work. From the nature of his injuries, it is believed that death must have been instantaneous. The unfortunate deceased has left a widow and large family of young children unprovided for.

The National Library of Scotland has the largest newspaper collection in Scotland, with copies of all Scottish titles and some of the main titles from across the UK. As well as original holdings the institution has many microfilms of newspapers which were photographed in 2000 as part of the NEWSPLAN 2000 Project, with almost four million pages imaged. These can be consulted within the building, and for a list of the titles which were microfilmed, visit **www.nls.uk/about/partnerships/newsplanscotland/titles.html**.

For more local holdings across Scotland, the library also has an online *Guide to Scottish Newspapers Indexes* at **www.nls.uk/collections/newspapers/indexes/index.cfm** which gives information on every newspaper which has been indexed, the years that have been covered, and the locations of the indexes. The index allows you to instantly see what exists, and provides details on how to pursue access for the records.

A slightly more unusual source from the library is *The Word on the Street* website, available at **www.nls.uk/broadsides**. Prior to modern day newspapers, people would get their news from single page 'broadsheets' which were posted on doors, posts and even trees, containing a mix of news and ballads. A collection of these has been digitised and made available on the site under key headings, though they are also fully searchable.

Many local authorities and individuals have also created specific indexes to births, marriages and death intimations from their local titles, such as those for local Perth and Fife titles (available also on the Ancestry website at www.ancestry.co.uk), for Ardrossan and Saltcoats in Ayrshire (see www.ayrshireroots.co.uk), whilst some are more ambitious such as Janice Halcrow's *Shetland Newspaper Transactions* site (www.jghalcrow.co.uk), which lists BMD intimation transcriptions from the *Shetland Times* from 1873 to 1900.

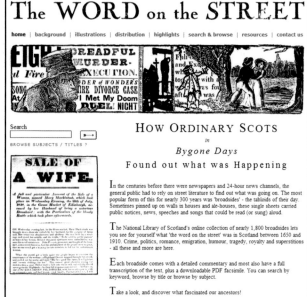

The National Library of Scotland has many useful newspaper resources online.

If you live further afield, there are five fully searchable digitised Scottish newspapers currently online which can greatly assist in your research. The first is the *Scotsman*, first established in Edinburgh in 1817. Initially responsible for covering the east coast, it is now one of the country's mainstream national papers. The online archive carries every edition of the paper from 1817 to 1950, and is accessible by subscription at http://archive.scotsman.com, with the cheapest pass available being for 24 hours access at £7.95.

Next up are three titles, the *Aberdeen Journal*, the *Glasgow Herald* and the *Caledonian Mercury*, available online as part of the British Library's 19th Century Newspaper Collection. These are accessible at http://newspapers.bl.uk/blcs for a subscription - £6.99 gives 24 hour access and a maximum of 100 articles to view, whilst £9.99 gives a week's access, and a maximum of 200 articles to view. The site also offers 19th century editions of two Irish titles, the *Belfast Newsletter* and the *Freeman's Journal*, and dozens of English and Welsh titles. Some academic and educational institutions also have subscriptions to the service.

Finally, an often ignored source is the free to access *Edinburgh Gazette*, the official paper of record for Scotland dating back to 1699, which is hosted at www.gazettesonline.co.uk. The paper is useful for identifying legal proceedings which may have affected your ancestors, such as sequestration (the Scots form of bankruptcy) and estates that have been disposed of after death, whilst it also deals with military matters such as army promotions, and civil awards such as the granting of knighthoods, OBEs etc.

Bear in mind that as part of the United Kingdom, stories from Scotland may also pop up in some of the nationals in England. Online British newspaper archives include *The Times* from 1785 to 1985 (**http://archive.timesonline.co.uk**), *The Guardian* and *The Observer* from 1791 to 2003 (**http://archive.guardian.co.uk**), and the *Daily Mirror* and *Daily Express* from 1900 to the present day (**www.ukpressonline.co.uk**).

Books

It may seem obvious, but don't forget to look in books! You will be surprised at how often your ancestor may appear in a volume, the problem is in trying to find those appearances. There are several online portals that have made this considerably easier in recent years.

The best site by far, and one which is constantly adding material by the day, is the mighty Google Books site at **http://books.google.com**. This contains absolutely everything and anything that Google has been able to get its hands on that is out of copyright or available in preview format, including specialised periodicals such as the Lancet, specific histories of an area, printed pedigrees and family histories, recent novels and historic classics, and so much more. Equally useful is the Electric Scotland website, where hundreds of books on a Scottish theme have been transcribed and/or digitised and placed online at **www.electricscotland.com/history/books.htm**.

Other sites worth exploring include the Universal Digital Library Million Book Collection at **www.ulib.org**, the Internet Archive Text Archive at **www.archive.org/details texts**, and Scribd at **www.scribd.com**.

There are also several online catalogues that can help you to locate a book that you may wish to consult, with the NLS catalogue at **www.nls.uk/catalogues/index.html** a useful starting point. Other online sources include the COPAC Academic and National Library Catalogue at **www.copac.ac.uk** for locations of books in British universities and libraries, whilst for elsewhere around the world, you can trace Scottish titles trough WorldCAT at **www.worldcat.org**, and the Library of Congress Online Catalogue at **http://catalog.loc.gov**.

Tip: Gateway Sites

There are of course far too many genealogical resources to list in one introductory guide, but there are several websites that act as gateways to other resources of genealogical use. One of the best is GENUKI Scotland, located at www.genuki.org.uk/big/sct, which lists dozens of useful website addresses arranged by both county and subject headings. It can occasionally be a bit temperamental and go offline, but there is a status site at www.genuki.info which flags up any potential problems. The Scottish pages of Cyndi's List at www.cyndislist.com/scotland.htm, and the Scotland's Family site at www.scotlandsfamily.com are both equally useful.

Photos

There are several websites carrying good online historic photographic collections. One of the best is the Scottish Cultural Resources Network (SCRAN) at **www.scran.ac.uk**, which has well over a million images and other media on the site, all drawn from various archive repositories across the country. There is a free search facility which returns thumbnail sized pictures, but to see full size images you will need to subscribe.

The Virtual Mitchell has an excellent collection of Glasgow street images at **www.mitchelllibrary.org**, whilst Alex Airlie's websites at **www.vintagescottish images.org.uk** and **http://secondcityoftheempire.moonfruit.com** carry useful images from across the country, but with a heavy emphasis again on Glasgow.

Dundee is well catered for at *Photopolis: Old Dundee in Photographs*, located at **www.dundeecity.gov.uk/photodb/main.htm**, whilst Edinburgh is well represented at **www.edinphoto.org.uk/0_a/0__photos.htm**. For other places in Scotland, **www. oldukphotos. com/scotland.htm** is also worth a visit.

The Scottish Highlander Photo Archive at **www.scottishhighlanderphotoarchive. co.uk** has hundreds of portraits and wedding photos depicting folk from the Highlands in the early 20th century, copies of which can be ordered up. When completed, it is estimated that some 20,000 images will be available on the site.

Emigration

There are many published sources for those seeking emigrant ancestors. For the United States and Canada, these include various passenger lists and immigration records found via Ancestry (**www.ancestry.co.uk**), whilst David Dobson has produced many useful series of books, including the seven volume *Directory of Scottish Settlers in North America 1625-1825*, with a full list available at **www.btinternet.com/~lds.dobson**. The hugely useful immigration site at Castle Garden **www.castlegarden.org** records immigrants arriving in the US between 1820 and 1892, whilst Ellis Island at **www.ellisisland.org** covers the later period from 1892 to 1924. For Canada, the Library and Archives Canada site at **www.collectionscanada.gc.ca** also has many immigration papers and censuses, whilst FindmyPast (**www.findmypast.co.uk**) also has a fantastic collection of passenger lists for those leaving the UK more recently between 1890 and 1960 for ports around the world.

The NAS has some limited collections, including papers from the Highlands and Islands Emigration Society (HD4/5) which helped people from 1851 to gain passage overseas, particularly to Australia, with a useful index to the collection held at the SCAN website at **www.scan.org.uk/researchrtools/emigration.htm**, showing names, residence and parish in Scotland of the applicant, ship name, ports' of arrival and departure, as well as dates of arrival and departure. A remarks column shows the amount paid for passage and a physical description which includes useful phrases such as 'appearance of great destitution' or 'strong healthy couple'. The archive also has papers from a state aided emigration scheme to Canada from 1886 to 1889 held under AF51.

Many Scots also ended up in India during the British Raj. Useful sites for Indian research include the many holdings of the National Library of Scotland (see Chapter 2), the Families in British India website (FIBIS) at **www.fibis.org**, and the British Library's India Office Family History Search page at **http://indiafamily.bl.uk**. An article on the Scots Cemetery in Kolkata appears in *Discover my Past Scotland* issue 5 (April 2009) available from **www.discovermypast.co.uk**, with many photos from the cemetery available at the CANMORE website from the RCAHMS at **www.rcahms.gov.uk/search.html**, though these are not yet indexed by name. FindmyPast.co.uk has various collections available for India also.

For New Zealand and Australia, there are again various sources via Ancestry of use, whilst the British Convict Transportation registers from 1787 to 1867 can be found at Queensland Government's website at **www.slq.qld.gov.au/info/fh/convicts**. The National Library of Australia's *Australian Newspapers* site at **http://newspapers.nla.gov.au** is another free to access treasure chest.

Poor Relief

Most of us will have an ancestor in our tree who has claimed poor relief at some stage. From 1845 the state took over responsibility for the administration of the poor from the Kirk, establishing a series of poor law unions across the country following the Poor Law Amendment Act. If a person lost his or her job and had no other means of support, he or she could claim temporary relief from the authorities. Long term cases were as-

The Glasgow City Archive has the best poor relief applications records in the country.

sessed and in many cases sent to the poorhouse (known as a 'workhouse' elsewhere in the UK). The authorities would make rigorous investigations into the applicant's social circumstances, in order to find somebody from whom they could reclaim the expense, and as such the records can often prove to be a genealogical goldmine.

Records are usually held in the local county records office, though a great many have not survived. The most comprehensive source showing what still exists can be found at the **www.workhouses.org** website, which also gives descriptions and photographs of many of the former poorhouse buildings still standing in Scotland.

The best surviving collection of poor law records in the country is that consisting of over a million poor relief applications for Glasgow (1851-1948), Barony (1861-1898) and Govan (1876-1930) which are held at Glasgow City Archives. A computerised index for these records up to 1901 is available within the archive room (though is sadly not online), and there are further records available for many other councils within Bute, Dunbartonshire, Lanarkshire and Renfrewshire. Online indexes exist for the records of many other areas, such as those compiled by the Friends of Dundee City Archives for Liff and Benvie (1854-1865) and Dundee's East Poorhouse (1856-1878), available at **www.fdca.org.uk/FDCADatabases.html**, and for Ardrossan at **www.threetowners. com/Ard%20folder/poor_application's.htm**. Some family history societies have also created CDs listing returns, such as those for Jedburgh from 1852-74, as transcribed by Borders FHS, with an online index naming all applicants held on its website (see Appendix 2).

Poor relief records can be extremely useful when researching ancestors who arrived from Ireland during the famine of the late 1840s, as they not only often contain information on other members of the family, but will also name from where in the country they originated. The authorities made strenuous efforts to unburden themselves from the massive drain on their finances caused by the sudden surge of Irish migrants from this period, and a useful list of people forcibly returned to poor law unions in their parish of origin in Ireland can be found through British Parliamentary papers. Many of these returns for 1867-69 and from 1875-78 have been made available at Raymond's County Down website (**www.raymondscountydownwebsite.com**).

For poor relief payments prior to 1845, you will need to consult the kirk session records (Chapter 4).

Hospital Records

There have been many types of hospitals in Scotland, including asylums and hospitals for the poor. If you are wishing to search for an ancestor who was hospitalised, be aware that patients' records are usually closed for a hundred years, and in some cases, the clinical records may not have in fact survived. The best starting point for your ancestral research is the Hospital Records Database at **www.nationalarchives.gov.uk/hospital records**. A collaboration between The National Archives at Kew and the Wellcome Trust, this lists over 2800 entries concerning the locations of hospital records held across Britain, though it is incomplete. A typical entry will tell you the name and location of the hospital, previous names and locations it may have had, the year it was founded, whether it is still in operation, and of course, the name of the archive or archives holding the institution's records.

Occasionally medical records will throw up some genealogical gems. Whilst researching the records of the Murray Royal Lunatic Asylum in Perth, for example, now held at the University of Dundee Archives, I came across a late 19th century book filled with genogram drawings, essentially a series of family tree diagrams recording the ancestral medical histories of many of the patients within the institution, often going back several generations.

Tip: Genograms

GenoPro is a software programme which allows you to go into considerable depth on both the medical and psychological factors within your family history. A guide on how its genogram charts work is available at www.genopro. com/genogram. A simpler programme to record medical family history with the purpose of identifying hereditary health risks is found online at the American based My Family Health Portrait site at https://familyhistory.hhs.gov/ fhh-web/home.action. Whilst professional genealogists rarely employ them, genograms are increasingly being used in the fields of medicine and family therapy.

Discussion forums

The *Rootschat* forum at www.rootschat.co.uk hosts a British wide discussion area with a very substantial Scottish section that allows users to post requests on ancestors within dedicated county based threads. In addition are various other threads for the rest of the United Kingdom, structured into the component countries, an area to advertise products, to swap merchandise, and much more.

The Canadian based Electric Scotland website, established by Alasdair MacIntyre, hosts a forum called *Aois* (Gaelic for 'age'), which is more of a Scottish history and cultural drop in site, handy for both members of the diaspora and indigenous Scots, and includes a genealogy section. The site is located at www.scotchat.org/vbull/ and even has its own virtual Scottish pub!

The *Talking Scot* forum at www.talkingscot.com is a basic discussion site with various threads on a range of subjects of Scottish interest, including a useful area for family history society contacts and some basic background details such as census dates etc. Registration is free. Another relatively new family history forum is that of the Scottish Catholic Archives, located within the family history section of its website at www.scottishcatholicarchives.org.uk, with useful discussion topics including Irish migration to Scotland, and Roman Catholic emigration to and from Europe.

Personally I find the best forum for Scottish research to be *ScotFamTree*, located at http://scotfamtree.11.forumer.com. Unlike the previously mentioned sites, there is a basic free Tier 1 subscription, followed by two tiers which require an annual subscrip-

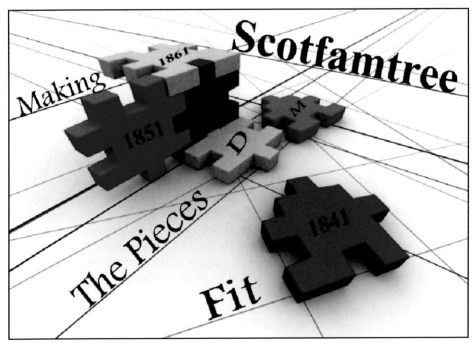

The ScotFamTree forum has its own online television channel.

tion of £8 to access. The advantage with a subscription is that the site hosts avidly collected research materials, some of which are transcribed or digitised, with permissions granted from various institutions for their use. In addition, the range of thread topics goes far beyond the offerings of other sites. As with Rootschat there are county based query threads, but also whole sections with threads on specific occupations, Irish research, a BMD exchange, and more. In essence the site acts as a virtual family history society, but at a considerably cheaper cost. As part of the site there is also a free to access online Scottish genealogy television channel at **www.livestream.com/scotlands familytreechannel** hosting many short films on topics of interest, some of which are produced overseas and some locally by members of the forum. The channel can also stream live forum based events, such as regular meetings of its members.

Further Reading

CAMPEY, Lucille H. (2008) *An Unstoppable Force: The Scottish Exodus to Canada.* Toronto: Natural Heritage Books.

CHRISTIAN, Peter (2009) *The Genealogist's Internet (4th edition).* London: The National Archives.

HEWITSON, Jim (1998) *Far Off in Sunlit Places: Stories of the Scots in Australia and New Zealand.* Edinburgh: Canongate.

WATERS, Colin (2009) *Family History on the Net: New Edition 2009-10.* Newbury: Countryside Books.

Afterword

If there is one thing that many people tend to forget when researching their ancestry, it is themselves! Your history is as important as that of any other member of your family, and there are many ways that you can add to the family story. One of the most useful is to try and keep a simple diary. It does not have to be elaborate, but if you can keep a note of some of the major events that happen in your life, even from time to time with brief updates, you will have in effect created a vital source that in a hundred years time will aid the next generation of genealogists within your family.

I first started keeping a diary at the age of 29, though bizarrely as a means to help with my learning of Scottish Gaelic – it seemed a great way to try and use the language, so for the first year I now have a record that no-one else in my family understands! Having realised just how useful a record it was becoming of my life, I then kept it regularly for the next six years (fortunately for the family, in English!), and it now has first hand accounts of my wedding day, the births of my two sons, the death of my grandmother and father-in-law and more. Whilst I no longer keep it on a daily basis, I do still update it monthly with any major happenings in our lives. There are other ways to achieve something similar. An uncle of mine in Melbourne, Australia, sends an annual newsletter to our family every Christmas, which lets us know how he and his clan are doing on the other side of the world.

Other valuable resources that you should think about trying to keep in order are photographs and video recordings. How many of us have piles of photos in boxes waiting to be sorted?! We may know who is featured in them, and what the occasion is, but unless you make a note on the back or keep them in an album, in fifty years these experiences will mean nothing to those who were not there.

Finally – a word of warning! I'd like to leave you with a bit of wisdom from my five times great uncle, Dr. William Henderson, as recalled in his 1870 book *Byegone Days; or, Sketches Illustrative of the Manners and Customs of the Scottish Peasantry Seventy Years Ago (by an Octogenerian)*:

> *In my estimation, a long line of ancestry entitles no man to trample on his brother, nor does a high sounding title give its possessor a right to wound the heart, which vibrates with the finer feelings of a common humanity, merely because accident has cast his lot in an elevated station of life, which he degrades by his vices, and in doing so prostrates the gifts of Providence, and makes them the means of wounding the peace and ruining the prospects of thousands, who though below him in station are nevertheless immeasurably raised above him in talent, in virtue, and proper feeling. Whether in prince or in peasant a genuine heart elicits from me the response of a brother.*

In other words, we're a' Jock Tamson's bairns! Family history is about self-discovery, and about having fun – please don't ever let it be about anything else!

Appendix 1. *Regional Archives*

The following is a list of regional and city archives found across Scotland. Many, though not all, have their collections catalogued on the Scottish Archive Network website at **www.scan.org.uk/catalogue**.

Aberdeen City Archives
(i) Old Aberdeen House, Dunbar Street, Aberdeen, AB24 3UJ
Tel: (01224) 481775 Fax: (01224) 495830
(ii)   Town House, Broad Street, Aberdeen, AB10 1AQ
Tel: (01224) 522513 Fax: (01224) 638556
[w]   **www.aberdeenshire.gov.uk/familyhistory/records.asp**
[e]   archives@aberdeencity.gov.uk

Angus Archives
Hunter Library, Restenneth Priory, By Forfar, DD8 2SZ
Tel: (01307) 468644
[w]   **www.angus.gov.uk/history/archives**
[e]   angus.archives@angus.gov.uk

Argyll and Bute Archives
Kilmory, Manse Brae, Lochgilphead, Argyll, PA31 8RT
Tel: (01546) 604774 or (01546) 604769
[w]   **www.argyll-bute.gov.uk/content/atoz/services/archives?s=0&a=0**
[e]   archives@argyll-bute.gov.uk

Ayrshire Archives
At the time of writing, Ayrshire Archives was relocating to temporary new premises at The Watson Peat Building, Auchincruive, Ayr KA6 5HW, from its previous home at the Craigie Estate, Ayr, KA8 0SS.
[w]   **www.ayrshirearchives.org.uk**
[e]   archives@south-ayrshire.gov.uk

Burns Monument Centre
Kay Park, Kilmarnock, East Ayrshire, KA3 7RU
Tel: (01563) 576695 or 576696   Fax: (01563) 576690
[w]   **www.burnsmonumentcentre.co.uk**
[e]   info@burnsmonumentcentre.com

Clackmannanshire Archives
Library Services, Library, Drysdale Street, Alloa, FK10 1JL
Tel: (01259) 722262
[w]   **www.clacksweb.org.uk/culture/archives/**
[e]   libraries@clacks.gov.uk

Dumfries and Galloway Archives
Archive Centre, 33 Burns Street, Dumfries, DG1 2PS
Tel: (01387) 269254   Fax: (01387) 264126
[w]   **www.dumgal.gov.uk/index.aspx?articleid=2300**
[e]   libarchive@dumgal.gov.uk

Dundee City Archives
21 City Square, Dundee, DD1 3BY
Tel: (01384) 434494   Fax: (01382) 434182
[w]   **www.dundeecity.gov.uk/archive**

East Dunbartonshire Archives
William Patrick Library, 2-4 West High Street, Kirkintlloch, G66 1AD
Tel: (0141) 7754574   Fax: (0141) 7760408
[w]   **www.eastdunbarton.gov.uk/Web+Site/Live/EDWebLive.nsf/**
          LU-AllContent/PBAD-5Q4J8J?OpenDocument
[e]   archives@eastdunbarton.gov.uk

East Lothian Archive Service
At the time of writing there are plans for a new purpose built archive facility at the John Gray Centre in Haddington.
Tel: (01620) 282229
[w]   **www.eastlothian.gov.uk/site/scripts/documents_info.php?documentID=534**
[e]   archives@eastlothian.gov.uk

Edinburgh City Archives
Level 1, City Chambers, High Street, Edinburgh EH1 1YJ
Tel: (0131) 5294616   Fax: (0131) 5294957
[w]   **www.edinburgh.gov.uk/internet/Council/Council_Business/**
          CEC_edinburgh_city_archives_2
[e]   archives@edinburgh.gov.uk

Falkirk Council Archives
Community Services, Calendar House, Callendar Park, Falkirk, FK1 1YR
Tel: (01324) 503779
[w]   **www.falkirk.gov.uk/services/community/cultural_services/museums/**
          archives/archive.aspx
[e]   callendar.house@falkirk.gov.uk

Fife Council Archives
Carleton House, The Haig Business Park, Balgonie Road, Merkinch, KY7 6AQ
Tel: (01592) 583352
[w]   **www.fife.gov.uk/topics/index.cfm?fuseaction=service.display&subjected =80607572-DA09-42F8-867CDC4CAD97EA4B&objectid=1E5C4D52-FCD7-40C7-8D76693F14B400E1**

Highland Council Archives
Inverness Library, Farraline Park, Inverness, IV1 1NH
Tel: (01463) 220330
[w]   **www.highland.gov.uk/leisureandtourism/what-to-see/archives/**
[e]   archives@highland.gov.uk

Lochaber Archive Centre
Lochaber College, An Aird, Fort William, Inverness-shire, PH33 6AN
Tel: (01397) 701942 or 700946
[w]   **www.highland.gov.uk/leisureandtourism/what-to-see/archives/ lochaberarchives/**
[e]   Lochaber.archives@highland.gov.uk

Local Heritage Services in Moray
East End School, Institution Road, Elgin, IV30 1RP
Tel: (01343) 569011
[w]   **www.moray.gov.uk/localheritage**
[e]   heritage@moray.gov.uk

North Highland Archives (serving Caithness)
Wick Library, Sinclair Terrace, Wick, Caithness, KW1 5AB
Tel: (01955) 606432   Fax: (01955) 603000
[w]   **www.highland.gov.uk/leisureandtourism/what-to-see/archives/ northhighlandarchives/**
[e]   north.highlandarchive@highland.gov.uk

Orkney Library and Archive
44 Junction Road, Kirkwall, Orkney, KW15 1AG
Tel: (01856) 873166
[w]   **www.orkneylibrary.org.uk/html/archive.htm**
[e]   archives@orkneylibrary.org.uk

Perth and Kinross Council Archive
A. K. Bell Library, York Place, Perth, PH2 SEP
Tel: (01738) 477012
[w]   **www.pkc.gov.uk/archives**
[e]   archives@pkc.gov.uk

Scottish Borders Archive and Local History Centre (The Heritage Hub)
Heart of Hawick, Kirkstile, Hawick, TD9 0AE
Tel: (01450) 360699
[w]   www.scotborders.gov.uk/council/specialinterest/heartofhawick/18964.html
         & www.heartofhawick.co.uk/heritagehub
[e]   archives@scotborders.gov.uk

Shetland Islands Museum and Archives
Hay's Dock, Lerwick, Shetland, ZE1 0WP
Tel: (01595) 741554
[w]   www.shetlandmuseumandarchives.org.uk/archiveCollections

Skye and Lochalsh Archive Centre
c/o Tigh na Sgire, Park Lane, Portree, Isle of Skye, IV51 9GP
NB: At the time of writing, the Skye and Lochalsh Archive Centre is planning to move
to to the new Skye & Lochalsh Archive Centre at The Elgin Hostel, Portree.
Tel: (01478) 613857
[w]   www.highland.gov.uk/leisureandtourism/what-to-see/archives/
         skyeandlochalsharchives/

Stirling Council Archive
5 Borrowmeadow Road, Stirling, FK7 7UW
Tel: (01786) 450745
[w]   www.stirling.gov.uk/index/access-info/archives.htm
[e]   archive@stirling.gov.uk

The Mitchell: Archives
Archives and Special Collections, The Mitchell, North Street, Glasgow, G3 7DN
Tel: (0141) 287 2910   Fax: (0141) 226 8452
[w]   www.glasgow.gov.uk/en/Residents/Library_Services/The_Mitchell/Archives/
[e]   archives@csglasgow.org

West Lothian Council Archives
9 Dunlop Square, Deans Industrial Estate, Livingston, EH54 8SB
Tel: (01506) 773770   Fax: (01506) 773775
[w]   www.westlothian.gov.uk/tourism/libservices/ves/
[e]   archive@westlothian.gov.uk

Appendix 2. *Family History Societies in Scotland*

The following is a list of Scottish family history societies. Most groups are members of the Scottish Association of Family History Societies (**www.safhs.org**).

Aberdeen and North East Scotland Family History Society
The Family History Shop, 164 King Street, Aberdeen, AB24 5BD
[w]   **http://anesfhs.org.uk**

Alloway & Southern Ayrshire Family History Society
c/o Alloway Public Library Doonholm Road, Alloway, AYR KA7 4RT
[w]   **www.asafhs.co.uk**

Borders Family History Society
30 Elliot Road Jedburgh TD8 6HN, Scotland
[w]   **www.bordersfhs.org.uk**

Caithness Family History Society
9 Provost Cormack Drive, Thurso Caithness, KW14 7ES, Scotland
[w]   **www.caithnessfhs.org.uk**

Central Scotland Family History Society
11 Springbank Gardens, Dunblane, FK15 9JX, Scotland
[w]   **www.csfhs.org.uk**

Dumfries and Galloway Family History Society
Family History Centre, 9 Glasgow Street, Dumfries, DG2 9AF, Scotland
[w]   **www.dgfhs.org.uk**

East Ayrshire Family History Society
c/o The Dick Institute, Elmbank Ave, Kilmarnock, KA1 3BU, Scotland
[w]   **www.eastayrshirefhs.org.uk**

Family History Society of Buchan
c/o Arbuthnot Museum, St Peter's Street, Peterhead, Aberdeenshire, AB42 1QD, Scotland
[w]   **www.fhsb.org.uk**

Fife Family History Society
Glenmoriston, Durie Street, Leven, Fife, KY8 4HF, Scotland
[w]   **www.fifefhs.org**

Glasgow & West of Scotland Family History Society

The Hon. Secretary, Unit 13, 32 Mansfield Street, Glasgow, G11 5QP, Scotland
[w]   www.gwsfhs.org.uk

Highland Family History Society

Suite 4, Third Floor, Albyn House, 37A Union Street, Inverness, IV1 1QA, Scotland
[w]   www.highlandfhs.org.uk

Lanarkshire Family History Society

26A Motherwell Business Centre Coursington Road, Motherwell, Lanarkshire,
ML1 1PW, Scotland
[w]   www.lanarkshirefhs.org.uk

Largs and North Ayrshire Family History Society

c/o Largs Library, 18 Allanpark Street, Largs, KA30 9AG, Scotland
[w]   www.largsnafhs.org.uk/home.htm

Lochaber and North Argyll Family History Group

c/o Fort William Library, Airds Crossing, Fort William, Lochaber, PH33 6EU
[w]   www.lochaberandnorthargyllfamilyhistorygroup.org.uk

Lothians Family History Society

The Hon. Secretary, c/o Lasswade High School Centre, Eskdale Drive, Bonnyrigg,
Midlothian, EH19 2LA, Scotland
[w]   www.lothiansfhs.org.uk

Moray & Nairn Family History Society

c/o Rivendell, Miltonduff, Elgin, Scotland, IV30 8TJ

Moray Burial Ground Research Group

c/o Rivendell, Miltonduff, Elgin, Scotland, IV30 8TJ
[w]   www.mbgrg.org

North Perthshire Family History Group

[w]   www.npfhg.org

Orkney Family History Society

Orkney FHS, Orkney Library & Archives, 44 Junction Road, Kirkwall Orkney,
KW15 1HG, Scotland
[w]   www.orkneyfhs.co.uk

Renfrewshire Family History Society

c/o 51 Mathie Crescent, Gourock, PA19 1YU, Scotland
[w]   www.renfrewshirefhs.co.uk

Shetland Family History Society
6 Hillhead, Lerwick, Shetland, ZE1 0EJ, Scotland
[w]   www.shetland-fhs.org.uk

Tay Valley Family History Society
Research Centre, 179-181 Princes Street, Dundee, DD4 6DQ, Scotland
[w]   www.tayvalleyfhs.org.uk

The Heraldry Society of Scotland
The Hon Secratary, 22 Craigentinny Crescent, Edinburgh, EH7 6QA, Scotland
[w]   www.heraldry-scotland.co.uk

The Scottish Genealogy Society
Library and Family History Centre, 15 Victoria Terrace, Edinburgh EH1 2JL, Scotland
[w]   www.scotsgenealogy.com

Troon @ Ayrshire Family History Society
c/o M.E.R.C. Troon Public Library, South Beach, Troon, Ayrshire, KA10 6EF, Scotland
[w]   www.troonayrshirefhs.org.uk

West Lothian Family History Society
Hon. Secretary, 23 Templar Rise, Livingstone, EH54 6PJ, Scotland
[w]   www.wlfhs.org.uk

Western Isles
The Western Isles and north west seaboard of Scotland have a series of historical societies known as 'comann eachdraidh' in Gaelic. The following are the main ones:

Comann Eachdraidh Barabhais agus Bhrù
(Baravas and Bru, Lewis)   www.barvasandbrue.com

Comann Eachdraidh Nis
(Ness, Lewis)   www.c-e-n.org

Comann Eachdraidh na Pairc
(Pairc, Lewis)   www.cepairc.com

Comann Eachdraidh an Taobh Siar
(West Side, Lewis)   www.ceats.org.uk

Comann Eachdraidh Uig
(Uig, Isle of Lewis)   www.ceuig.com

Comann Eachdraidh Muideart
(Moydart)   www.moidart.org.uk

Comann Eachdraidh Lios Mor
(Lismore)   **www.celm.org.uk**

Comann Eachdraidh Bharraidh agus Bhatarsaidh
(Barra and Vatersay)   **www.barraheritage.com**

Comann Eachdraidh Bhearnaraigh
(Berneray)   **www.isleofberneray.com/groups/historical.html**

Comann Eachdraidh Bheinn na Foghla
(Benbecula)   **www.benbeculahistorysociety.co.uk**

Comann Eachdraidh Eige
(Isle of Eigg)   **www.isleofeigg.net/heritage/society.htm**

Comann Eachdraidh Ghleann Lìomhann
(Glenlyon)   **www.glenlyon.org**

Comann Eachdraidh Loch Ròg an Ear
(East Loch Roag)   **www.breasclete.com/Groups/comanneachdraidh.html**

Comann Eachdraidh Shlèite
(Sleat, Skye)   **www.sleatlocalhistorysociety.org.uk**

For Western Isles research, it is also advisable to contact the *Co Leis Thu?* genealogy resource based at the Seallam! centre at Northton on the Isle of Harris, which has researched almost every household in the Outer Hebrides for the last two centuries. Written records are quite recent in the Western isles, but the Gaelic oral tradition contains a great deal of genealogical information, and is amongst the centre's prized possessions. For more information, visit **www.seallam.com/coleisthu.htm**.

Index